TULIPS

TULIPS

AN ILLUSTRATED IDENTIFIER AND GUIDE TO CULTIVATION

Stanley Killingback

CHARTWELL
BOOKS, INC.

A QUINTET BOOK

Published by Chartwell Books
A Division of Book Sales, Inc.
110 Enterprise Avenue
Secaucus, New Jersey 07094

ISBN 1-55521-704-4

This book was designed and produced by
Quintet Publishing Limited
6 Blundell Street
London N7 9BH

Creative Director: Terry Jeavons
Designer: Nicky Chapman
Project Editors: David Barraclough,
Lindsay Porter
Photographer: Cathy Wilkinson Barash
Illustrator: Vana Haggerty

Typeset in Great Britain by
Central Southern Typesetters, Eastbourne
Manufactured in Hong Kong by
Regent Publishing Services Limited
Printed in Hong Kong by
Leefung-Asco Printers Limited

CONTENTS

INTRODUCTION

This book aims to refer briefly to all the essential aspects of the tulip and its growth, but the emphasis is directed to assisting the general gardener to add colour to the garden, to delight the eye and lift the spirit. The tulip is probably more widely grown and popular than any other flower except the rose, and this fame has now lasted for over three centuries. Millions of words have been written about the tulip, but a high proportion of the best known books on the subject were written 50 or more years ago and during that period there has been a complete revolution in the types and classes of tulips grown. Throughout this book I have divided the tulips into the classes or sections of the latest classified list shown in chapter 2. But classification has been changed in almost every edition and may well change again soon.

No book about flowers can ever be completely up-to-date. I have always written notes on the tulips I have grown and these are often rapidly outdated. In 1966 I grew over one hundred blooms of the single early tulip 'Bellona' as the perfect foil for the red Darwin hybrids, especially 'Oxford', and my note says it was the best golden yellow for this purpose, blooming year after year on the same day as 'Oxford'. Two years later I was growing 'Golden Oxford', which is the same colour as 'Bellona' but is larger, taller, easier to grow and would soon be much cheaper.

Many gardeners select their bulbs from a coloured reproduction of the flower they wish to grow. This largely ignores the fact that some tulips resent certain types of soil or situation.

A selection of catalogues from which tulips can be ordered.

~

I have been growing tulips for 42 years. In that time I have grown some 350,000 blooms in 760 varieties and have gradually become more and more obsessed with this flower. The obsession is now complete and everything else in my average-sized garden has to take second place. Inevitably I think that all tulips are beautiful, though some are much more beautiful than others and, while sympathizing, cannot concur with Sir Daniel Hall's 'nightmares' quoted in chapter 3. I also tend to favour those cultivars which thrive in my local soil, a heavy clay. This should be considered by anyone aiming to grow tulips.

With any flower one must develop personal preferences. Mine will probably show themselves through the writing, so I may as well bring them out now. I prefer and grow mostly the very early botanical tulips, with some mid-season and very few lates. The first reason is that the early flowers shorten the winter. It is a constant joy to me to walk out into the garden in early spring, or in some years late winter, and see a blaze of bright colour. My second reason is that I grow flowers for garden decoration. Almost all my tulips are lifted every year. The gaps so left must be filled with summer bedding. There is little time for this when the late tulips are ready to lift. These are also the ones I most like.

Throughout the book I have used the word 'robust' to mean strong-growing, tough, sturdy and the word 'vigorous' to mean producing many offsets, bulbils or stolons. The abbreviations used are listed on this page.

I should like to acknowledge my debt to all those who have raised and introduced the tulips that I have so much enjoyed, to the RHS, the KAVB, the Directors and staff of Wisley and Kew Gardens and to all those who have written informatively and entertainingly about tulips, especially Sir Daniel Hall, Wilfred Blunt, Tom Lodewijk and Zinaida Botschantzeva.

Finally, I have had countless hours of intense pleasure from growing tulips and I hope that this book may assist many others to share in the joy that they can give.

Stanley Killingback

ABBREVIATIONS

FCC	First Class Certificate
AM	Award of Merit
HC	Highly Commended
H	Haarlem/Hillegom (from 1971)
W	Wisley/RHS
TBV	Tulip breaking virus
RHS	Royal Horticultural Society, London
KAVB	Koninklijke Algemeene Vereeniging voor Bloembollencultuur (Royal General Bulbgrowers' Association, Hillegom)

ORIGINS

The well-documented history of the garden tulip starts only in 1554 when bulbs and seeds arrived in western Europe from Turkey. The Belgian diplomat Ogier de Busbecq (1522–92), envoy of the Holy Roman Emperor to Suleiman the Magnificent, referred to 'tulipam', which had little or no smell but were admired for the beauty and variety of their colours. Busbecq sent seeds and bulbs to Vienna. Only five years later Conrad Gesner saw tulips in the gardens there. Two years later they were seen growing in Augsburg and the following year a merchant in Antwerp received a cargo of bulbs from Constantinople. From Flanders the tulip was introduced into Holland and from there, throughout Europe.

It must be emphasized that the tulips that came from Turkey in 1554 were not wild flowers. Instead they were highly cultivated products. Without a doubt, they reached the consumer as the results of experimentation, expertise and experience. The first seedlings from these bulbs comprised all kinds of varieties, early, late and mid-season, and with the colour range known today. Except for minor points of shape and size, modern garden tulips still possess no important characteristics which were not present in the original introduction. There is every indication that these tulips had been cultivated for centuries, but there is no evidence that this took place in Turkey. Suggestions have been made that they originated in the ornamental gardens of Baghdad in Iraq, but it seems more probable that they came from Persia where the word for tulip, 'lale', is the same as the Turkish word. It is clear that Busbecq must have misunderstood when he said the Turks called them 'tulipam'. He could have heard the Turkish word 'tülbent' (turban) being used to describe tulips. The Persian poet Musharrifu'd-din Sa'di, describing a garden in his poem Gulistan, in 1258, wrote:

> *The murmur of a cool stream*
> *Bird song, ripe fruit in plenty,*
> *Bright multi-coloured tulips and fragrant roses.*

The word 'multi-coloured' suggests that they were either variegated tulips or garden tulips raised from different coloured species. In either case they would be cultivated garden tulips since only garden tulips are susceptible to the tulip breaking virus.

There is still absolutely no link for the transition from a wild flower to a cultivated garden flower. For centuries botanists and gardeners were seeking this link and for a long time it was attributed to *Tulipa gesneriana,* which was in any event a collective name given by Linnaeus for a large number of ancient cultivars. It appears at present to be a totally mythical attribution.

Certainly in Persia there were many poems written long before there is any evidence that the flower was available in Turkey. In Persia the tulip became the symbol of perfect love, especially red tulips with a black centre.

ARRIVAL IN ENGLAND

Tulips reached England in about 1578. About four years later the Englishman Richard Hakluyt (cousin of the compiler of *Voyages*) wrote of various flowers named 'tulipas' that were then being imported from Austria by an excellent man called Carolus Clusius.

The tulip soon became popular in England. Gerrard, in his famous *Herball* (1597), tells us that his 'loving friend master James Garratt . . . a curious searcher of simples, and learned

apothecary in London' had been experimenting for 20 years with different kinds of tulips in a very large number of varieties.

Then in 1629 the famous horiculturist John Parkinson wrote his *Paradisus,* perhaps the greatest gardening book in our language. He was the first English author to do full justice to the tulips. He enumerates 140 varieties 'all now made denizens in our gardens, where they yield us more delight and more increase for their proportion than they did unto their own naturals . . . but indeed this flower, above many other, deserveth his true commendation and acceptance with all lovers of these beauties, both for the stately aspect, and for the admirable variety of colours that daily does arise in them'.

For a time the fame of the tulip eclipsed that of the rose and the daffodil. John Tredescant, gardener to Charles I, grew 50 varieties in his garden, and the taste of the Court was eagerly imitated. Although tulips are not mentioned by Shakespeare or Milton, Herrick mentions them in 'the sadness of things for Sapho's sickness'. Marvell also loved the tulip.

Rubens and his wife in their garden at Antwerp *(Peter Paul Rubens, c1632). Painted when tulipomania was at its height, the rectangular plot through the wooden gate contains tulips.*
~

TULIPOMANIA

The tulip was late in reaching France, where the religious wars had preoccupied men. There is no record of a tulip flowering here until 1608. But soon after this no woman of fashion would be seen in the spring without a bunch of tulips tucked into her low cut dress. Within a few years bulbs were changing hands for fantastic sums.

The craze for spending enormous sums on tulips spread northwards through Flanders (where Rubens was busy painting his second wife Helena Fourment in her new tulip garden) to Holland, where it became a total mania.

'Tulipomania' had little to do with the tulip as such and certainly did not advance the history of the tulip. It was simply a series of gigantic gambles which, like the South Sea Bubble and the Mississippi Company, ended in national disaster. It was the habit of the tulip when inflicted by virus of breaking into sometimes beautiful variegated forms that implemented the gambling. It often started in quite a small way. Anyone who had a few yards of back garden could grow bulbs, and the outlay was small for a few breeder tulips. The prizes if you obtained a winning broken or rectified tulip could be enormous.

Tulipomania was at its height between 1634 and 1637, although it did not entirely die out until 1642. Sometime before this the enthusiasm of Dutch amateurs had already forced the prices of rare bulbs up to a ridiculous figure. The most famous of the broken tulips was one called 'Semper Augustus', with a red and white flower and pointed petals. Some 'Semper Augustus' bulbs were sold for thousands of florins in 1623.

In this heady period tulip growing went hand in hand with speculation. People of every description joined the merchants in speculating. At first everyone won and no one lost. Then as the gamble grew wilder, the stakes grew higher, houses and estates were mortgaged.

In every town in Holland a collegium or club for tulip trading was set up in a chosen tavern. It was illegal to offer bulbs for sale but this was soon got round by elementary negotiation. In the early days sales took place between the end of June, when the bulbs were all lifted, and September, when replanting was started. Later deals were made all the year round, even when bulbs were still in the ground. Later still, speculators would often pay large sums for a root which they never expected to receive and others sold roots which they never possessed or delivered. Very often a tulip never actually changed hands. A buyer would buy and sell and sell again. The bulb – without changing hands – was often sold four, five or more times.

During the tulip season more bulbs were traded on this basis than in all probability were to be found in all the gardens of Holland. It was pure speculation, of a sort normally found in a stock exchange. It was trading in something as elusive as the wind and it did in time come to be called the wind trade. Many people threw themselves into it with reckless abandon, showing no concern for their future. Many lives and fortunes were ruined.

Few fortunes were made, but those that did best out of their involvement in the wind trade were the innkeepers. It was in their establishments that most of the transactions were carried out.

The bubble finally burst on the 3 February, 1637. A number of merchants who were buying and selling bulbs at an inn decided to test the market prices. The price for a pound of tulips gradually dropped and they realized that the bottom had fallen out of the market. Prices were still high in many areas for a number of years but the main speculation was now over.

TENDER BEAUTY	
Classification	Darwin hybrid
Year introduced	c1951
Height	20in/50cm
Awards	AM W 54

TULIPA SPECIES

As has been mentioned the first tulips to come to western Europe were cultivated garden tulips. Then a number of wild tulip species started arriving in the Netherlands. In many cases the true geographical origins of these species have become obscure. Most of them, however, seem to have come from a corridor close to latitude 40° north. They are prevalent in the area from Armenia to the Tian-Shan mountain range, separating China from the Soviet Union. But there are certainly some found in Turkey, Iraq and Iran.

Some of these species have later been described as being wild in western Europe. For example, *T. australis* and *sylvestris* and *T. oculus solis* have been found apparently wild in Italy, southern France and Savoy, but if they were truly indigenous to these areas surely they would have been mentioned either in literature or become apparent in figurative art. In their European habitats these tulips have an erratic distribution, generally in cultivated land. This suggests introduction by human agency rather than truly wild growth.

CLUSIANA	
Classification	Species
Height	10in/25cm

Another consideration affects *T. clusiana*, at one time described as the Persian tulip. It now appears to be indigenous in several European locations, notably in Spain. But it does not set seed and increases only by stolons. So it seems almost certain that it must

have been propagated vegetatively and has been distributed in Europe by man since it was introduced in 1606.

These are just a few of the many problems confronting the botanists and gardeners who wish to seek the origin of the garden tulip. At present no wild tulips have been found which – even when hybridized together – would have formed the vast range of cultivated garden tulips we now know.

Keukenhof, Lisse, in Holland.
~

TULIPS SPREAD ACROSS THE WORLD

The popularity of the tulip in England, Holland, Flanders and northern France increased rapidly in the eighteenth century. Dutch and Flemish artists loved the tulip. Ambrosius Bosschaert's *A vase of flowers in a window,* made up of splendid tulips, must be regarded as one of the supreme flower paintings of all time.

Many important books were published. Parkinson's was one of the first. Then came Monstereul's *Le Floriste François* (1654), an exhaustive work dealing with the culture of the tulip; Van Oosten's *The Dutch Gardener* (1703), in which tulips were given first place; and Le Père d'Ardene's classic *Traite des Tulipes* (1760). Van Oosten calls the tulip the queen of flowers and states that tulips should be widely available so that everyone can get the benefit of their beauty.

Meanwhile the poets were again noticing the tulip. The references by Lord Byron and in the *Rubaiyat of Omar Khayyam* were almost certainly to the wild tulip, but Tennyson, Robert Browning, Elizabeth Barrett and Rupert Brooke are certainly referring to the garden tulip. Who can forget Brooke's nostalgic cry from Berlin in 1912:

Here tulips bloom as they are told

Meanwhile in Turkey something very close to a mania relating to the tulips developed from 1703 onwards. It never degenerated into a financial swindle as in Holland. Instead, it was much closer to being a genuine obsessive love of the flower itself.

A major change was taking place in Flanders and in the northern cities of France such as Lille. Here a new race of breeder tulips were being grown which were broadly cup-shape but with a much squarer base. The Flemish and Lille growers were extremely competent and their bulbs commanded the highest prices. Towards the end of the nineteenth century all but one of the famous Flemish tulip collections had disappeared. The one that remained, Lenglart, was put up for sale because its owner was too elderly to care for it. The Haarlem grower E. H. Krelage purchased the Lenglart collection because he saw that its monochrome breeder tulips would serve as the foundation of a new type of tulip. He was able to develop just such a new class and call them Darwins.

In 1850 Alexandre Dumas had published a popular novel, *La Tulipe Noire,* which betrayed his ignorance of botany. Two years after introducing the Darwins, Krelage introduced a purple black variety which he called 'La Tulipe Noire'. It is still in cultivation.

During the early years of the twentieth century the tulip bulb industry began to expand enormously in Holland and it attracted many visitors. Keukenhof, near Lisse was established in 1949. There bulbs could be shown throughout the season and in greenhouses even out of season. Each year enormous crowds attend the 'corso', or flower festival, held in the bulb region near Haarlem.

Madame Lefeber in Monticello, Virginia, USA.
~

TULIPS IN NORTH AMERICA

Tulips have an enormous following in the United States, which can perhaps be attributed in part to the influence of Dutch settlers. There are certainly a number of tulip festivals held throughout the country, particularly in those areas where a high proportion of the population is of Dutch origin. Among the best are those held in Holland, Michigan, Pella and Orange City, Iowa; and Albany, New York. But arguably the greatest North American display of tulips takes place in Canada's capital city, Ottawa. Once again, links with Holland have been influential: after Holland's Queen Juliana gave birth in the Ottawa Civic Hospital, the Dutch began sending tulips to Ottawa every year. A spring festival celebrating the tulip is also held in the middle of May.

NCC Gardens in Ottawa, Canada.
~

Although many problems remain regarding the origins of the garden tulip, it enters the last decade of the century in a very promising situation. New cultivars are always coming along and old ones are well tended. The tulip faces a very thriving and promising future.

Dance
~

REGISTRATION AND CLASSIFICATION

I n the sixteenth century, Rembertus Dodonaeus (1517–85) lists tulips as early, mid-season and late. This division is still used in the Classified List, organized by the Royal General Dutch Bulb Growers' Society (KAVB), with help from the Royal Horticultural Society. It is clear, however, that Dodonaeus used the word 'mid-season' primarily as meaning late-blooming early tulips and the early-blooming lates. During the next few centuries the early tulips were divided into singles and doubles and the late tulips were divided primarily into English breeders, Dutch breeders and the various florists' tulips mentioned in Chapter 6. Later came the parrot and cottage tulips, originally tulips found in cottage gardens. Later most tulips that did not fit into other categories were placed in the cottage division.

At first early tulips were defined as those that bloomed before 21 April in the Thames Valley. Later the Duc van Tol tulips were added. These flowered about a fortnight earlier but were primarily used only for forcing.

Then, about 100 years ago, E. H. Krelage of Haarlem purchased the entire stock of a race of tulips bred mostly in Flanders but partly in Lille. He gave them the name of Darwin. They were essentially tulips with a more cup or goblet-shaped bloom. For centuries until then tulips had been regarded as a rich man's flower because the expensive florists' tulips had dominated the market. Around the time of the wide introduction of the new Darwin tulips it became fashionable to see breeder or self-coloured flowers. They also were very much cheaper.

As a result, at the beginning of this century the number of new tulips rose dramatically, and with it the number of synonyms employed. Some tulips had as many as six synonyms, which proved a genuine obstacle to proper trading. In 1913 the Royal Horticultural Society decided to set up an Anglo-Dutch committee in order to straighten out the naming and classification of tulips and eliminate synonyms.

The Tulip Nomenclature Committee first sat in 1914 under the chairmanship of E. A. Bowles. The vice-chairman was E. H. Krelage and the other members were J. de Graaff, T. Hoog, Jan Roes, P. R. Barr, C. W. Nedham, A. D. Hall, W. T. Ware, G. W. Leak, the Rev. Joseph Jacob and later R. W. Wallace. The trials officer was C. C. Titchmarsh.

An immense number of tulips were requisitioned from growers in England and Holland and these were grown as trials at Wisley in the spring of 1915. Cut blooms were sent to the RHS Hall where they were judged and examined by the committee. Unfortunately, by this time the war prevented the Dutch growers from joining the committee, but they subsequently examined the recommendations in their own country. A long report showing the names of tulips and the synonyms to be eliminated was published by the RHS in 1917 and the following classification was suggested:

Early Flowering	1	Duc van Tol
Section 1	2	Single Early
	3	Double Early
May Flowering	4	Cottage
Section 2	5	Dutch Florists
	6	English Florists
	7	Darwin
	8	Broken Dutch
	9	Broken English
	10	Rembrandt (broken Darwins)
	11	Broken Cottage
	12	Parrot
	13	Late Double
Section 3	14	Species of tulipa

Tulip bed in Wisley Gardens.
~

During the next 10 years many new cultivars were introduced. Darwins predominated, but there were also two new races of tulips. Mendels were the result of crossing Duc van Tol with Darwin. Triumph tulips were obtained by crossing single earlies with May-flowering tulips. With these introductions it occurred that synonyms were again being used and names employed for more than one cultivar. In 1923 the Royal Horticultural Society again appointed a Tulip Nomenclature Committee. E. A. Bowles presided once more. There was close cooperation between the RHS and the Royal General Dutch Bulb Growers' Society. From 1929 onwards a number of extensive trials were carried out in Haarlem.

In 1929, before these trials were completed, the RHS decided to publish a tentative list of tulip names. In 1930 it added a supplement to the tentative list. The classification in these two lists followed exactly that of the 1917 report.

In 1939 the first full classified list was published by the RHS. It added full mid-season classification, including Mendel and Triumph tulips. The only other change to the previous list was that the Dutch and English Florist tulips were renamed Dutch and English breeder tulips. In 1948 a new classified list was published by the RHS, this time in association with the Royal General Dutch Bulb Grower's Society. The classification was unchanged but those cottage tulips known to have a lily-flowering shape were specially marked and it was agreed that in some future list they would be given a separate classification.

The third full classified list was published by the RHS in association with the KAVB. The list was unchanged apart from the addition of Darwin hybrid tulips as a separate section.

In 1955 the 14th International Horticultural Congress was held at Scheveningen and the International Committee on Horticultural Nomenclature Registration discussed in detail the functions and method of operation of international registration authorities. The KAVB accepted the invitation to be the international registration authority for tulips and some other hardy bulbs. Since that time the classified lists have all been published by the KAVB.

A bed of Darwin hybrids.
~

The first list they published was in 1958 and the two groups of breeder tulips were united into one. There was also a new classification for lily-flowering cultivars and the Darwin hybrids were given a place of their own, though they were still classified as late tulips. The subdivision of broken breeders or cottage were given the historic name Bizarre tulips if striped on a yellow ground and Bijbloemen tulips if striped on a white ground. However the principal change in the scheme was the expansion given to the division of species and first crosses between species. These gave special sections to eichleri, fosteriana, greigii, kaufmanniana, marjolettii and to the varieties and hybrids of batalinii and tubergeniana. A further space was given to all other species. All these changes were approved by a meeting held in Haarlem in December 1956 between delegates of the RHS and of the KAVB.

Bulbwalk at Sissinghurst, Kent.
~

There were no changes in the 1963 edition of the list, but in the 1969 edition it was decided that only the kaufmanniana, fosteriana and greigii sections of these species should have their own classification. The remainder were all included in other species. At the same time the Darwin hybrid tulips were transferred to the mid-season flowering section and the Duc van Tol were included in the single earlies and the breeder tulips were amalgamated with the cottage division except for a few which according to their shape were placed in either the Triumph or Darwin section. Finally the Rembrandt, Bizarre and Bijbloemen tulips were amalgamated into one division and called Rembrandt tulips.

This edition also decided to include all the names of sports beside the original parent, and synonyms of the botanical species were excluded. The 1976 edition of the classified list retained the 1969 classification.

In 1981 the Mendel tulips were eliminated, the earlier blooming varieties being included with the single earlies and the later ones were amalgamated with the Triumphs. At the same time the Darwin and cottage tulips were amalgamated into one section now known as Single Lates. Those cottage tulips with green stripes or markings and those with fringed edges were separated into two new sections called Fringed and Viridiflora. This was the same classification used in the latest list, dated 1987. This is the latest classification list as we have it.

CLASSES OF TULIP	
Earlies	1 Single Early
	2 Double Early
Mid-season	3 Triumph
	4 Darwin Hybrid
Lates	5 Single Late
	6 Lily-Flowered
	7 Fringed
	8 Viridiflora
	9 Rembrandt
	10 Parrot
	11 Double Late (peony flowered)
Species	12 Kaufmanniana
	13 Fosteriana
	14 Greigii
	15 Other species

DANCE	
Classification	Fosteriana
Year introduced	1952
Height	10in/25cm
Awards	AM W 54

The 1987 list did state that the Rembrandt section would be closed as there were now virtually no tulips being grown commercially under this heading. But I have just been told by the KAVB that the class Rembrandt tulips is not to be replaced by any other class as this class still has historical importance.

The Committee for the Registration of Tulip Names will be meeting towards the end of 1990 and it is anticipated that the next classified list will probably be published in 1991.

Anyone raising a new tulip and wishing to have it registered must send some bulbs to the KAVB for testing in the trial grounds of the association. Entry forms are obtainable from the Royal General Dutch Bulb Growers Association (KAVB), Parklaan 5, Hillegom, Holland.

Ibis

EARLY TULIPS
SINGLE AND DOUBLE

The term 'early tulips' is traditional rather than real these days. It goes back virtually to the introduction of the tulip to western Europe. Early tulips are mentioned by Dodonaeus in the sixteenth century, and since that time there has always been a group of tulips called single earlies. At the beginning of this century early tulips were classified as those that bloomed before 21 April in the Thames Valley. Today even most mid-season tulips bloom before that date in that area. One of the latest of the single early tulips, called 'Couleur Cardinal', blooms at virtually the same time as the early cottage tulips, let alone the mid-season. In the present classification, with the elimination of Mendel tulips, many of the single earlies were in fact mid-season tulips only a few years ago.

Twelve of the first 20 tulips I ever grew were single earlies, and one was a double early. When the Darwin hybrids were first offered for sale they were virtually all red. I grew over 100 bulbs of single early 'Bellona' because it associated with them so well. For several years I noted that it bloomed on exactly the same day as 'Oxford', my favourite red Darwin hybrid. Then 'Golden Oxford' appeared and 'Bellona' immediately became obsolescent for me. The larger and taller 'Golden Oxford' was the same colour and bloomed on the same day as 'Bellona'. I knew it would eventually be cheaper, as indeed it now is.

The early tulips – both single and double – produce the overwhelming majority of those tulips suitable for forcing. A list is given in chapter 12.

SINGLE EARLIES

Many of the oldest tulips in cultivation fall into this class. 'Keizerskroon' is carmine scarlet deeply edged golden yellow, and 'Prince Carnival' is yellow flamed red. 'Keizerskroon' is one of the very oldest tulips in the classified list, being in cultivation since 1750. Other very old early tulips are 'Yellow Prince' (1785) and 'Silver Standard' (1637). Many more of these varieties, such as the forcing tulip 'Brilliant Star', were introduced in the latter half of the nineteenth century. Most of the single early tulips are between 10 and 15 inches (25–40 cm) high. A number of them are stated to be scented, but that seems to be an exaggeration.

FRAGRANT TULIPS

The tulips below are stated to be more fragrant when cut and taken indoors, but 'Golden Show' is sweetly scented anywhere.

'Bellona' (Gold)
'Doctor Plesman' (Orange-red)
'Ellen Willmott' (Primrose)
'General de Wet' (Orange)
'Peach Blossom' (Pink)
'Prince of Austria' (Orange-red)
'Sylvestris' (Yellow)

'Keizerskroon' and 'Prince Carnival' are not the only good bi-coloured tulips. 'Sunburst' is yellow flushed red, 'Crown Imperial' is purplish brown edged dull yellow and 'Ibis' is a beautiful deep rose shading to silvery white at the edge. Perhaps better still is 'Pink Beauty, which is white in the centre edged bright glowing deep rose. Other good pinks are 'Proserpine' and 'Pink Perfection'. Excellent scarlets are 'Cramoisi Brilliant', 'Charles' and 'Doctor Plesman'. 'White Hawk' and 'Diana' are good whites, and there are several good yellows, including 'Joffre', 'Yokohama' and 'Ursa Minor'. 'Christmas Marvel' is a good cherry pink, 'Christmas Gold' is a deep canary yellow and 'Merry Christmas' is chrysanthemum crimson. 'General de Wet' is an excellent fiery orange colour and 'Princess Irene' is a soft orange with salmon and buff featherings. Three more recent bi-colours should be mentioned. 'Montparnasse', red flamed yellow, is a sport of the excellent 'Bellona'. 'Mickey Mouse', yellow flamed red, is a sport of 'Winter Gold'. Even more recent is 'Flair' (1978), which has a long red flame on the buttercup yellow ground, and is feathered Dutch vermilion.

IBIS	
Classification	Single
Year introduced	1910
Height	12in/30cm
Awards	AM W 14

PRINCE CARNIVAL	
Classification	Single early
Year introduced	1930
Height	13in/32.5cm

KEIZERSKROON	
Classification	Single early
Year introduced	1750
Height	14in/35cm

PINK

TULIPS IN THE PINK, ROSE, SALMON COLOUR RANGE

CLASSIFICATION GROUP	NAME	DATE	COLOUR	AWARDS	HEIGHT
1	Apricot Beauty	1953	soft apricot-rose		16in/40cm
1	Jenny	1980	cyclamen pink		16in/40cm
2	Peach Blossom	1890	bright pink	AM H 13	10in/25cm
3	Billboard	1978	flamed neyron-rose		18in/45cm
3	Don Quichotte	1952	tyrian-rose		18in/45cm
3	New Design	1974	pinkish-white/apricot		18in/45cm
4	Big Chief	1959	rose-madder	AM H 60. FCC W 69	26in/65cm
4	Pink Impression	1979	Empire-rose		24in/60cm
5	Mirella	1953	salmon	FCC H 61. AM W 67	25in/62.5cm
5	Clara Butt	1889	buff-rose	FCC W 05	24in/60cm
5	Queen of Bartigons	1944	salmon	FCC H 61. FCC W 53	24in/60cm
5	Rosy Wings	1944	radiant pink	AM H 47	23in/57.5cm
6	Mariette	1942	satin pink	FCC H 50. AM W 68	23in/57.5
6	China Pink	1944	radiant pink		20in/50cm
7	Burns	1968	phlox-pink		20in/50cm
7	Belleflower	1970	rose-bengal		20in/50cm
10	Fantasy	1910	salmon-pink	FCC H 22. AM W 21	22in/55cm
11	Angelique	1959	pale pink		16in/40cm
11	Eros	1937	old rose	AM H 37	22in/55cm
12	Jeantine	1952	carmine-pink		8in/20cm
12	Heart's Delight	1952	red/white/pink	HC W 66	8in/20cm
13	Spring Pearl	1955	vermilion-pink		18in/45cm
13	Sylvia van Lennep	1965	deep pink		18in/45cm
14	Toronto	1963	coral pink		12in/30cm
14	Roseanna	1952	pink/red/white		16in/40cm
14	Perlina	1960	porcelain-rose		10in/25cm
15	*pulchella* Eastern Star	1975	magenta-rose		4in/10cm

APRICOT BEAUTY	
Classification	Single early
Year introduced	1953
Height	16in/40cm

For me the most important members of single early class are those that have colours that cannot be bettered in any other early or mid-season tulip. The popular 'Van der Neer' is the outstanding older tulip. It dates from 1860 and is a glowing purple. There are also a number of tulips which until a few years ago were classified as Mendel tulips. Outstanding among these is 'Apricot Beauty', in a colour very difficult to describe. It is a delicate shade of soft apricot rose, very faintly tinged with red and with a slightly richer colour in the interior. Although this is not the most robust of tulips, its beauty makes it an essential. It has three excellent sports. 'Bestseller' is a bright coppery orange, 'Jenny' is a deep cyclamen pink fading almost to white at the edges and 'Beauty Queen' is feathered empire rose on a salmon ground with a shrimp red midrib, inside scarlet with a greenish yellow base. All these sports are beautiful, but like their parent they are not the most robust and should be given special treatment.

DIANA	
Classification	Single early
Year introduced	1909
Height	11in/27.5cm
Awards	AM H 14

BESTSELLER	
Classification	Single early
Year introduced	1959
Height	16in/40cm

PRINCESS IRENE	
Classification	Single early
Year introduced	1949
Height	13in/32.5cm

EARLY DOUBLES

This is probably the most controversial section of all. Many people love these double early tulips, others tend to look on them with disdain. Sir Daniel Hall, director of the John Innes Horticultural Institute, in his *Book of the Tulip* (1929) wrote 'the doubling of a flower is always a doubtful blessing, but to double a tulip is to destroy the finest and most distinctive qualities that it should possess. It may be argued the double tulips are more lasting, but it is no gain that a nightmare should endure for two nights instead of one'. Although I have some sympathy with Sir Daniel's view, he has an equally obdurate objection to the double late or peony-flowered tulips, and here I do not think I can agree. Some of the peony flowered tulips are quite attractive, and they are certainly much more robust than the early doubles.

Double tulips were first mentioned in histories in 1665, but it was nearly two centuries later before any significant information became available about the early doubles. The dominant feature of this class of tulip is 'Murillo' and its many sports. Raised in 1860, 'Murillo' has produced no less than 101 sports in a very wide range of colours. Some of its sports are stated to be blooming earlier than the original but I have not discovered any of these on sale. Probably one of the attractions is that you can have a large number of tulips, all exactly the same apart from the wide range of colours. The sports of 'Murillo' are in all shades of pink, red, yellow and orange and even the deep violet purple of 'David Tenniers'. They all grow about 10 in (25 cm) high and bloom outdoors in mid-April. Some of the more popular of these sports include 'Peach Blossom' (bright pink), 'Orange Nassau', 'Goya' (salmon scarlet and yellow), 'William Kordes' (cadmium orange) 'Williamsoord' (carmine and white), 'Mr van der Hoef' (yellow), 'Paul Crampel' (scarlet), 'Electra' (deep cherry red) and as previously mentioned, 'David Tenniers' (deep violet purple).

PEACH BLOSSOM	
Classification	Double early
Year introduced	1890
Height	10in/25cm
Awards	AM H 13

SCHOONOOLD	
Classification	Double early
Year introduced	c1906
Height	10in/25cm
Awards	FCC H 09

ORANGE NASSAU	
Classification	Double early
Year introduced	1930
Height	10in/25cm

Leaving the somewhat controversial 'Murillo' and its many sports on one side, arguably the best of the double earlies is 'Scarlet Cardinal'. This is a vivid and bright scarlet shaded orange flower of similar stature to the 'Murillos', but it has a forcing time of 10 December. Another good red is 'Stockholm', whilst 'Monte Carlo' is a good sulphur. One of the smallest, if not the smallest, in this group is 'Baby Doll'. It is a deep buttercup yellow and has a height of only 8 in (20 cm). Two rather taller varieties which bloom at the end of April are 'Carlton', which is a deep turkey red about 12 in (30 cm) high, and 'Hoangho', which is a pure yellow with a very good stem and a height of 14 in (35 cm). Gardeners must decide for themselves whether they like these double earlies. It is reasonable to recommend that a start should be made with 'Scarlet Cardinal', which in my opinion, is certainly the best of this classification.

ELECTRA	
Classification	Double Early
Year introduced	1905
Height	10in/25cm
Awards	FCC H 12

MONTE CARLO	
Classification	Double early
Year introduced	1955
Height	16in/40cm

BABY DOLL	
Classification	Double early
Year introduced	1961
Height	8in/20cm

SCARLET CARDINAL	
Classification	Double early
Year introduced	1914
Height	10in/25cm
Awards	AM H 15

Ivory Floradale
~

MID-SEASON TULIPS

lthough mid-season tulips were mentioned by Dodonaeus (1517–1585), they were not really a classification of tulips. Instead they included those early tulips that bloomed later than usual and the late ones that bloomed earlier. Mid-season tulips proper developed between 1917 and 1927 with the introduction of the Mendel and Triumph tulips. Mendels were the result of crossing 'Duc van Tol' cultivars with Darwin tulips, and Triumph tulips were obtained by crossing single early cultivars with May-flowering tulips. However, most of the new varieties were still under trial in Holland when the first issue of the classified list appeared in 1929. Mid-season tulips as such were not part of the classified list until 1939. In 1952 the Darwin hybrids were given a classification of their own, but they were placed after the Darwin tulips as lates, and it was not until the 1969 edition that they were transferred to the mid-season section. After this the Mendel tulips were eliminated as a classification, the early-flowering ones becoming single early tulips and the later-flowering ones becoming Triumph tulips.

DARWIN HYBRIDS

The original Darwin hybrid tulips were the result of crosses between Darwin tulips and *Tulipa fosteriana*. They now include the result of crosses between other tulips and botanical tulips, which have a similar habit and in which the wild plant is not evident. Many of the early Darwin hybrids were raised by D. W. Lefeber and introduced during the Second World War. 'Holland's Glory', 'Lefeber's Favourite', 'Dardenelles' and 'Red Matador' appeared in 1942. 'Holland's Glory' was the favourite of many people, but in the early days its high price limited its popularity. Almost all the early Darwin hybrids were red and of these the favourite of D. W. Lefeber was 'Oxford', introduced in 1945.

The first non-red Darwin hybrid was 'Oranjezon', usually called 'Orange Sun'. It was introduced in 1947, and originally classified as a Triumph tulip. 'Oranjezon' was not transferred to the Darwin hybrid section until many years later. The first non-red introduced as a Darwin hybrid was 'Gudoshnik' (1952). 'Orange Goblet' and 'Big Chief' arrived in 1959, and 1960 brought 'Vivex'. Since those days, mutations of the original plants have given mostly golden sports, but there have been other striped and edged sports of many of the original reds.

ORANGE SUN	
Classification	Darwin hybrid
Year introduced	1947
Height	22in/55cm
Awards	AM H 64

Of the original red tulips I favour 'Oxford', because when lifted it gives an excellent new bulb for next year's flowering together with a reasonable number of offsets. Its chief rival 'Apeldoorn', gives more offsets but fewer large bulbs when lifting. 'Apeldoorn' is the favourite of the professional growers, whether supplying bulbs or supplying cut flowers, but for the ordinary gardener I think that 'Oxford' has the edge. It also blooms several days earlier than 'Apeldoorn' and is therefore right in the centre of the mid-season. 'Lefeber's Favourite' is a beautifully shaped bloom, but it is one of the latest to bloom and is somewhat smaller, about the size of 'Diplomate'. 'London' and 'Dover' are also excellent reds, though 'Dover' tends to open very wide in the sun and consequently does not last quite so long as some of the others. The vigorous 'Red Matador' was probably the first Darwin hybrid to come along in an extremely cheap form. It has one snag: it has to be planted rather early, otherwise it tends to come blind. 'Spring Song' opens slightly pinkish but soon turns to a good red and it is probably the best in this section for naturalizing. An excellent red with a very beautiful shape is 'Canopus', originally classified fosteriana and later transferred to Darwin hybrid. These days it does not appear to be on sale. In the early days a very popular large variety was 'General Eisenhower'. This seems to have been almost completely superseded by 'Empire State', which is similar to 'Oxford' but a little larger and taller. They bloom at the same time and go well together. Finally there is 'Parade', which is also large and opens quite wide.

BIG CHIEF	
Classification	Darwin hybrid
Year introduced	1959
Height	26in/65cm
Awards	AM H 60 FCC W 69

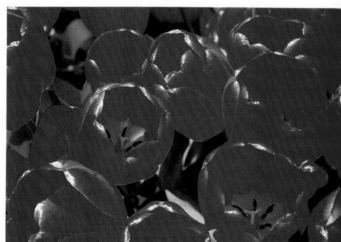

OXFORD	
Classification	Darwin hybrid
Year introduced	1945
Height	24in/60cm
Awards	AM H 53 FCC W 78

RED

CLASSIFICATION GROUP	NAME	DATE	COLOUR	AWARDS	HEIGHT
	TULIPS IN THE RED COLOUR RANGE				
1	Brilliant Star	1906	scarlet	FCC H 08	10in/25cm
1	Merry Christmas	1972	chrysanthemum crimson		15in/37.5cm
2	Scarlet Cardinal	1914	scarlet	AM H 15	10in/25cm
3	Paul Richter	1945	geranium-lake	AM W 78	18in/45cm
4	Empire State	1956	signal-red	FCC H 60. FCC W 69	24in/60cm
4	Oxford	1945	scarlet	AM H 53. FCC W 78	26in/65cm
4	Parade	1951	signal-red	AM H 53. FCC W 78	24in/60cm
5	Halcro	1949	salmon-carmine	FCC H 64. AM W 77	28in/70cm
5	Landseadle's Supreme	1958	cherry red	FCC H 61. FCC W 77	26in/65cm
5	Renown	1949	light carmine	FCC H 51. AM W 68	26in/65cm
6	Dyanito	1949	glowing red	FCC H 51	24in/60cm
7	Arma	1962	cardinal-red		12in/30cm
7	Burgundy Lace	1961	wine-red	AM W 70	26in/65cm
7	Redwing	1972	cardinal-red		18in/45cm
7	Sundew		cardinal-red	AM H 30	22in/55cm
10	Red Champion	1930	glistening red		18in/45cm
10	Vesuvius	1962	scarlet		10in/25cm
11	Uncle Tom		maroon	AM H 39	20in/50cm
12	Scarlet Baby	1962	scarlet		8in/20cm
12	Showwinner	1966	cardinal-red		9in/22.5cm
13	Cantata		orange-red		11in/27.5cm
13	Madame Lefeber		oriental red	FCC H 32	18in/45cm
14	Majestic	1970	scarlet	AM H 42	22in/55cm
14	Oriental Beauty	1952	blood-red		12in/30cm
15	*eichleri*		scarlet	AM H 39. AM W 70	10in/25cm
15	*linifolia*		scarlet	AM H 32. AM W 70	5in/12.5cm
15	*praestans* Turbergen's Variety		orange-scarlet		12in/30cm
15	*turbergeniana* Keukenhof	1952	scarlet		22in/55cm

Many of these red Darwin hybrids have produced golden or yellow sports. My own favourite is 'Golden Oxford'. Others include 'Golden Apeldoorn', 'Golden Parade', 'Golden Empire State', 'Golden Springtime' and 'Jewel of Spring', an excellent sulphur yellow sport of 'Gudoshnik'. It is very vigorous and will naturalize very well. 'Oxford' and 'Apeldoorn' in particular have produced a number of other sports, of which probably the most important are 'Oxford's Elite' and 'Apeldoorn's Elite' with an exterior of red edged orange yellow inside feathered and spotted red on an orange yellow ground. The two are somewhat similar apart from the obvious differences between the parents. Two sports of 'Apeldoorn' are quite unusual. 'Apeldoorn's Favourite' is a glowing scarlet semi-double, whereas 'Exotic Bird' has a red cyclamen shaped flower.

GOLDEN SPRINGTIME

Classification	Darwin hybrid
Year introduced	1957
Height	25in/62.5cm
Awards	FCC H 60 FCC W 69

JEWEL OF SPRING

Classification	Darwin hybrid
Year introduced	1956
Height	24in/60cm
Awards	AM H 60 FCC W 78

DAYDREAM

Classification	Darwin hybrid
Year introduced	1980
Height	24in/60cm

SPRING SONG

Classification	Darwin hybrid
Year introduced	1946
Height	24in/60cm

MY LADY	
Classification	Darwin hybrid
Year introduced	1959
Height	24in/60cm
Awards	AM H 61 HC W 69

Some varieties in this section are either orange or very close to orange. The most perfect is 'Orange Sun', stated to be the purest orange seen in any tulip. It blooms later than most of the others.

'Vivex' is officially deep carmine rose edged orange yellow with a star-shaped base deep green on yellow ground, but certainly its appearance is orange. 'Orange Goblet' is described as mars-orange with a yellow base and has an extremely large flower. It is, however, less free-flowering than many others. 'Queen Wilhelmina' (strictly 'Koningin Wilhelmina') is scarlet edged orange both inside and out, but the overall effect is certainly one of an orange colour. It is a sport of 'Lefeber's Favourite'. An interesting cultivar is 'Daydream'. It is a sport of 'Yellow Dover'. When it first opens it is identical to 'Yellow Dover', but gradually an orange flush comes over the flower and before it dies it is completely orange in colour. At a distance, 'Oxford's Elite', 'Beauty of Oxford', 'Apeldoorn's Elite' and 'Beauty of Apeldoorn' do have a slightly orange appearance.

'Holland's Glory' mentioned earlier is a good red and is now within the price range of most people. Although it is officially a dazzling scarlet, I have always felt that it had a hint of orange. It soon gave a very beautiful sport, 'My Lady', which is vivid coral orange. Another excellent orange, introduced in 1985, is 'Lighting Sun'. It is an excellent marigold tulip with a slight flush of azalea pink on the exterior. A sport of 'Orange Sun', it was wrongly classified in 1987 as a single late. I am assured by Hillegom that this will be rectified in the next classified list.

ORANGE

TULIPS IN THE ORANGE COLOUR RANGE

CLASSIFICATION GROUP	NAME	DATE	COLOUR	AWARDS	HEIGHT
1	Bestseller	1959	coppery-orange		16in/40cm
1	Princess Irene	1949	orange/salmon		13in/32.5cm
3	Orange Monarch	1962	orange		18in/45cm
3	Showmaster	1965	deep orange	AM H 64	18in/45cm
4	Lighting Sun	1985	marigold-orange		24in/60cm
4	My Lady	1959	vivid coral-orange	AM H 61. HC W 69	24in/60cm
4	Orange Sun	1947	pure orange		22in/55cm
4	Vivex	1960	orange with rose		25in/62.5cm
5	Dillenburg	1916	orange terracotta	FCC H 37	26in/65cm
6	Marjolein	1962	orange and rose	AM H 82	23in/57.5cm
10	Orange Parrot	1942	orange	AM H 50	24in/60cm
11	Orange Triumph	1944	orange-red	AM H 44	20in/50cm
12	Early Harvest	1966	reddish-orange	AM H 73	8in/20cm
12	Love Song	1966	reddish-orange		8in/20cm
13	Juan	1961	pale orange		16in/40cm
13	Orange Brilliant	1962	Indian-orange		19in/47.5cm
13	Orange Emperor	1969	carrot-orange		20in/50cm
13	Toulon	1961	deep orange	HC W 66	15in/37.5cm
14	Orange Elite	1952	orange/rose	AM W 66	10in/25cm
14	Orange Toronto	1988	pure orange		12in/30cm
15	*praestans* Isaphan		orange		12in/30cm
15	*vvedenskyi* Tangerine Beauty	1900	orange/buff/yellow		5in/12.5cm

DAWNGLOW	
Classification	Darwin hybrid
Year introduced	1965
Height	24in/60cm

PINK IMPRESSION	
Classification	Darwin hybrid
Year introduced	1979
Height	24in/60cm

There are some excellent Darwin hybrids in which pink is the predominant colour. 'Dawnglow' is a pale apricot flushed carmine with a hint of orange on the interior, a beautiful combination of colours that is not easy to describe. Being a sport of 'Red Matador', raised from fosteriana crossed with Mendel, it needs to be planted reasonably early to give a good show. An even larger tulip is 'Big Chief', which is rose madder edged orange-red, also with a good flush of orange on the inside. This is a very good bedding variety, but it will not take kindly to being left in the ground or naturalized. 'Elizabeth Arden' is an excellent rose pink. Until recently classified as a Darwin, it is rather shorter and smaller than most Darwin hybrids. However there are not all that many pinks and this one has been essential. The best pink of all, 'Pink Impression', was produced in 1979. On the outside it is veined empire rose on pale rose ground with a neyron rose flame and a broad shrimp red feathered edge. Inside it is a bright claret rose on a pale rose ground with a black base and small yellow edge. Being relatively new it is still priced a little above most Darwin hybrids, but it is a good buy.

There are no whites in this section, although one could use 'Purissima', which has a similar parentage to 'Red Matador' (Mendel × Fosteriana). The nearest to white is 'Ivory Floradale', which is ivory yellow on the outside and creamy yellow on the inside and maybe slightly spotted carmine red.

IVORY FLORADALE	
Classification	Darwin hybrid
Year introduced	1965
Height	24in/60cm

There are three sports, which are yellow with stripes or flushes of red. 'Dutch Fair' is buttercup yellow ribbed scarlet and is a sport of 'Dover'. 'Olympic Flame', a sport of 'Olympic Gold' is mimosa yellow flamed deep red. 'Flaming Gold' is buttercup yellow flamed red and is a sport of 'Franklin D. Roosevelt'.

Finally I come to 'Tender Beauty', in my opinion the most beautiful tulip in this section. With a strong stem carrying a huge flower of white edged rosy red with a yellow base, it is outstanding but despite being in cultivation for nearly 40 years it is still extremely expensive and will almost certainly remain so for the rest of its days. It is one of the few tulips that is a tetraploid.

Darwin hybrid tulips are now to be seen everywhere – in private gardens, public gardens and parks. This is not surprising since they are so robust, vigorous and extremely cheap.

OLYMPIC FLAME	
Classification	Darwin hybrid
Year introduced	1971
Height	21in/52.5cm

TRIUMPH TULIPS

In the years following the First World War, Triumph tulips were introduced in considerable numbers. They are a cross between a single early and a May-flowering tulip. They are robust although perhaps slightly less vigorous than the Darwin hybrids. But they have a much greater range of colour. Triumphs did not appear in the classified list until 1939. In 1981 their numbers were considerably increased by the transfer of all later flowering Mendel tulips. A number of earlier flowering cottage tulips, notably 'Carrara', were also transferred. It is perhaps in the violet purple range of colours that these tulips are so valuable. Arguably the most beautiful of all is 'Blue Orchid' (purple violet in colour), but the most popular is probably 'Attila', a light purple violet. There are several others: 'Purple Queen' (brilliant tyrian purple), 'Purple Marvel' (lilac purple), 'Purple Star' (purple) and 'Prince Charles' (purple violet). 'First Lady' is reddish violet flushed purple, 'Emmy Peeck' is a deep lilac rose and 'Anne Claire' is magenta rose. A more recent introduction is 'Negrita' which is doge purple veined beetroot purple. 'Arabian Mystery' is a deep purple violet edged white and 'Dreaming Maid' is violet edged white.

PRINCE CHARLES	
Classification	Triumph
Year introduced	1952
Height	18in/45cm
Awards	AM W 57

ARABIAN MYSTERY	
Classification	Triumph
Year introduced	1953
Height	18in/45cm

ATTILA	
Classification	Triumph
Year introduced	1945
Height	20in/50cm

DREAMING MAID	
Classification	Triumph
Year introduced	1934
Height	20in/50cm

There are several good whites in this section, possibly the best is 'Carrara', formerly a cottage tulip. 'Kansas', 'Hibernia' and 'Pax' are also good. There are also a number of good pinks in this section. An old favourite is 'Peerless Pink', a pure satin pink. Another old variety, 'Pink Glow' is a satin rose. 'Don Quichotte' (tyrian rose) and 'Douglas Bader' (amaranth rose and china rose on white) are excellent. A newer one is 'Billboard', which is flamed neyron rose with a small red edge.

HIBERNIA	
Classification	Triumph
Year introduced	1946
Height	19in/47.5cm

Many of the reds and yellows appear to have been superseded by the Darwin hybrids of a similar colour, but there are still some that are well worth growing. 'Alberio' is cherry red with a creamy edge and is the sport parent of so many of the parrot tulips. 'Robinea' is a good cardinal red and the brownish red 'Cassini', though fairly old, is still extremely vigorous. 'Paul Richter' is the former Darwin tulip transferred to the Triumph class. It is the best of the later tulips for forcing. Of the yellows, 'Golden Melody' is a buttercup yellow, 'Reforma' is a sulphur yellow and 'Ornament' is a large egg-shaped yellow. But above all I must mention 'Golden Show', which is a deep yellow with a very large flower. It is the most strongly scented of all the tulips that I have grown.

There are several good orange tulips in this section: 'Adorno' (salmon orange), 'High Society' (orange red edged pure orange), 'His Highness' (clear bronze tinged orange throughout) and 'Mary Housley' (apricot orange). 'Orange Monarch' is orange with a slight pink tinge but the orange tulip that has performed best for me is 'Showmaster', a deep orange with a yellow edge.

MERRY WIDOW	
Classification	Triumph
Year introduced	1942
Height	13in/32.5cm
Awards	AM H 43

LUCKY STRIKE	
Classification	Triumph
Year introduced	1954
Height	16in/40cm

Among the bi-colours, 'Elmus', 'Edith Eddy', 'Merry Widow' and 'Lucky Strike' are good red and whites. 'Aureola', 'Golden Eddy' and 'Kees Nelis' are good red and yellows, as is 'Princess Beatrix'. An excellent tyrian rose with a hint of purple edged white is 'Valentine'. These are also two with somewhat unusual colouring. 'Abu Hassan' is a glowing cardinal red with crysanthemum stripes on a small buttercup yellow edge. 'Madame Spoor' is a mahogany red edged yellow. These two go well together. 'Fidelio' is magenta-edged orange.

There are a number of white tulips with a pink edge, possibly the best known are 'Meissner Porzellan', a very pleasing shade of rose and white, and 'Garden Party', white with a glowing pink edge and white base. Another good one is 'Her Grace', but in my garden the most successful has been 'Akela', an excellent white with a pink edge, and a robust grower. It is fairly new, being raised in 1980.

KEES NELIS	
Classification	Triumph
Year introduced	1951
Height	15in/37.5cm

VALENTINE	
Classification	Triumph
Year introduced	1970
Height	20in/50cm

FIDELIO	
Classification	Triumph
Year introduced	1952
Height	19in/47.5cm

Other newer Triumphs that have given me a great deal of pleasure are 'Annie Schilder' (1982), a mixture of empire rose and Indian orange, and 'New Design'. This opens Naples yellow but fades to a pinkish white with a pale fuschian red margin. Inside it is Naples yellow with apricot flame and a buttercup yellow base. The green leaves have a notable pinkish white margin showing quite a deep pink when they first come through, but fading to pinkish white. Finally there is 'Happy Family' (1985), which is not only a very attractive rosein pink but is also a multi-flowering or branching tulip.

The Triumph tulips are an excellent race. They are mostly extremely robust and reasonably vigorous and they give an excellent show, mostly towards the end of April. They are a very large family and I strongly recommend that they should be introduced into every garden.

ABU HASSAN	
Classification	Triumph
Year introduced	1976
Height	20in/50cm

Gander
~

LATE TULIPS
SINGLE AND DOUBLE

ate tulips have been mentioned since the first tulips were brought from Turkey into western Europe. At the outset they were mostly singles; the doubles came along about 1665.

SINGLE LATE TULIPS

This is a very large list, comprising the popular Darwin tulips together with most of the cottage tulips and both the Dutch and English breeder tulips. Against these additions to the list, the lily-flowering and later the fringed and viridiflora tulips have been taken out of the list.

Usually the first bloom is 'Mirella', a beautiful tulip of unusual shading. It has a long oval head with buff rose petals and a broad flame of raspberry red rising from the base. Inside it is silver rose shading through carmine to a black blue base. 'Mirella' is a sport of 'Advance', which appears to have been superseded by the late-flowering Darwin hybrids. But 'Mirella', with its great beauty, remains popular. The first early Darwin to appear is the ever popular 'Demeter', a rich plum purple variety. 'The Bishop' is an excellent violet purple, 'Dorie Overall' is dark petunia violet edged mauve and 'Cum Laude' is dark campanula violet. 'Cleopatra' is purple and 'Madame Butterfly' is violet purple. 'General Patton' is a deep lilac, 'Bleu Aimable' is a beautiful deep mauve shaded purple and 'Greuze' is a dark violet purple.

'La Tulipe Noire' is a deep purple black, and its fame has derived as much from the novel by Alexandre Dumas as from its own quality. 'Queen of the Night' is a deep velvet maroon and 'Black Diamond' is a dark reddish brown on the exterior and a dark dahlia purple inside. Both of these varieties look black at a distance. Two cultivars are classified as absolutely black: 'Black Beauty' and 'Black Pearl'.

'Gander' is a bright magenta and is an excellent bedding and forcing variety. Its sport, 'Red Gander', is cardinal red on the outside and currant red on the inside.

Pinks

There are many pinks in this section. Probably the most famous and most popular is 'Clara Butt', a soft, bright salmon pink. Many professionals argue that 'Queen of Bartigons' is the best of

ARISTOCRAT	
Classification	Single late
Year introduced	1935
Height	24in/60cm
Awards	AM H 38

all. It is also a pure salmon pink and is a sport of 'Bartigon'. 'Cantor' is a soft coral pink; 'Aristocrat' is a clear magenta pink with a light edge and very large flowers. 'Pink Supreme' is a very delicate bright pink, lighter towards the edges, and 'Princess Elizabeth' is rose. 'Palestina' is much shorter than most single late tulips but it has large flowers and a colour combination of salmon and rose. 'Rosy Wings' is a radiant pink and a very long flower of a very distinct shape almost lily-flowering. Finally 'Smiling Queen' is a deep, pure pink, a well-shaped flower and very long lasting.

Reds

Two tall, robust and vigorous introductions by Segers Brothers must be mentioned. 'Halcro' is a deep salmon carmine with a yellow base and a large oval-shaped flower. 'Renown' is a light carmine red with a yellow base and also with large oval-shaped flowers. 'Renown' has two excellent sports: 'Avignon' is spinel red and 'Menton' is China rose with light orange stripes on the edge and poppy red with a white vein inside. Another excellent red is the long-lasting 'Landseadle's Supreme', a glowing cherry red on a strong stem. 'Scarlet Leader' is blood red and 'King's Blood' is cherry red edged scarlet. 'Flying Dutchman' is currant red and 'Musical' is cardinal red. 'Tel Aviv' is raspberry red and 'Balalaika' is a large glowing turkey red.

ROSY WINGS	
Classification	Single late
Year introduced	1944
Height	23in/57.5cm
Awards	AM H 47

HALCRO	
Classification	Single late
Year introduced	1949
Height	28in/70cm
Awards	FCC H 64 AM W 77

PURPLE

TULIPS IN THE PURPLE, VIOLET, MAUVE COLOUR RANGE

CLASSIFICATION GROUP	NAME	DATE	COLOUR	AWARDS	HEIGHT
1	Van der Neer	1860	purple		10in/25cm
2	David Tenniers	1960	violet-purple		10in/25cm
3	Attila	1945	purple-violet		20in/50cm
3	Blue Orchid	1942	purple-violet		18in/45cm
3	Purple Queen	1970	tyrian-purple		20in/50cm
3	Negrita	1970	doge-purple		18in/45cm
5	Demeter	c1930	plum-purple	AM H 32	27in/67.5cm
5	Bleu Aimable	1912	lilac	AM H 16	24in/60cm
5	Cleopatra	1960	purple		25in/62.5cm
5	The Bishop	1908	violet-purple		25in/62.5cm
5	Madam Butterfly	1930	violet-purple	FCC H 38	25in/62.5cm
6	Burgundy	1957	purplish-violet		19in/47.5cm
6	Maytime	1942	reddish-violet		19in/47.5cm
7	Blue Heron	1970	violet-purple		26in/65cm
7	Canova	1971	cobalt-violet		24in/60cm
10	Blue Parrot	1935	violet/purple	AM H 35	24in/60cm
10	Muriel	1961	violet		16in/40cm
11	Blue Flag	1750	light violet		16in/40cm
11	Lilac Perfection	1951	lilac		18in/45cm
11	Clara Carder	1943	tyrian-purple	AM H 50	18in/45cm
15	*bakeri* Lilac Wonder	1971	rosein-purple	FCC H 77	6in/15cm
15	*pulchella humilis*	1982	violet-purple		4in/10cm
15	*pulchella violacea*		purple-red		4in/10cm

RENOWN	
Classification	Single late
Year introduced	1949
Height	26in/65cm
Awards	FCC H 51 AM W 68

BALALAIKA	
Classification	Single late
Year introduced	1952
Height	20in/50cm

LANDSEADLE'S SUPREME	
Classification	Single late
Year introduced	1958
Height	26in/65cm
Awards	FCC H 61 FCC W 77

Yellows

'Golden Harvest', a well-established variety, is a large citron yellow. 'Bingham' is a good golden yellow. 'Fortune's Gift' is a good maize yellow, edged rose.

Whites

'Maureen' has long oval flowers of white flushed ivory. 'Sigred Undset' is creamy white. 'Snow Peak' is pure white. There are three good whites with coloured edges. 'Blushing Bride' is creamy white edged red, 'Magier' (Magician) is a fine milky white edged soft purple and 'Shirley' is white with a narrow edge of soft purplish blue, lightly spotted with the same colour.

WHITE

TULIPS IN THE WHITE, IVORY COLOUR RANGE

CLASSIFICATION GROUP	NAME	DATE	AWARDS		HEIGHT
1	Diana	1909	AM H 14		11in/27.5cm
1	White Hawk	1880			12in/30cm
3	Carrara		AM H 12	FCC W 22	20in/50cm
3	Pax	1942			18in/45cm
5	Maureen	1950	FCC H 56	AM W 60	20in/50cm
5	Sigrid Undset	1954	AM H 54		26in/65cm
5	Snowpeak	1952		FCC W 57	26in/65cm
6	White Triumphator	1942		HC W 82	28in/70cm
7	Swan Wings	1959		AM W 70	22in/55cm
0	White Parrot	1943			20in/50cm
1	Mount Tacoma	1926	FCC H 39		22in/55cm
3	Purissima	1943	AM H 49		20in/50cm
3	Concerto				10in/25cm
5	*biflora*				7in/17.5cm
5	*turkestanica*				9in/22.5cm

MAGIER

Classification	Single late
Year introduced	1951
Height	26in/65cm

SHIRLEY

Classification	Single late
Year introduced	1963
Height	24in/60cm

PRINCESS MARGARET ROSE	
Classification	Single late
Year introduced	1944
Height	22in/55cm

Bi-colours

'Rosa van Lima' is lilac rose edged salmon red; 'Silver Wedding' and 'Sweet Harmony' are both yellow edged white. 'Arizona' is buttercup tinged red and 'Pandion' is purple edged white.

There are a number of cultivars remaining from those found growing in English cottage gardens. Possibly the best known of these is 'Inglescombe Yellow' (W. T. Ware). It is a triploid, has won awards of merit in England and Holland and was the first tulip I grew. Although a little shorter than many in this section, it is robust and vigorous and will naturalize anywhere. It has several good sports, 'Princess Margaret Rose' (yellow edged orange-red). 'Lincolnshire' (vermilion) and 'Vlammenspel' Fireside (yellow flamed scarlet) as well as some parrot tulips.

Some of the most interesting colour combinations belong to the old tulips, formerly called breeder tulips. These range from purple to bronze-orange, yellow and buff. 'Louis XIV' is bluish violet with a tawny margin. 'Dillenburg' is orange terracotta 'Southern Cross' is lemon yellow edged orange. 'George Grappe is lavender blue and 'Jan van Galen' is raspberry and orange 'Fulton' is purple edged bronze and 'Mount Royal' is a glowing bluish purple edged bronze-orange. Many of these old breeder tulips were also very tall. Certainly the tallest tulip that I have ever grown was the breeder tulip 'Jessy' (chestnut brown flushed violet), which in my garden grew up to 40 in (one metre) regularly.

'Scaramouche' (purple edged bronze-yellow) would appear to be in the breeder class but is in fact a sport of 'Golden Harvest'. Other interesting colours are 'Beverly' which is orange red and 'Bond Street' which is yellow and orange. A complete chart of bicolour tulips is on pages 66 and 67.

PANDION	
Classification	Single late
Year introduced	c1950
Height	24in/60cm
Awards	FCC H 54 AM W 57

DILLENBURG	
Classification	Single late
Year introduced	1916
Height	26in/65cm
Awards	FCC H 37

SWEET HARMONY	
Classification	Single late
Year introduced	1944
Height	22in/55cm
Awards	FCC H 47 AM W 55

BLUSHiNG BEAUTY	
Classification	Single late
Year introduced	1983
Height	26in/65cm

YELLOW

TULIPS IN THE YELLOW, GOLD COLOUR RANGE

CLASSIFICATION GROUP	NAME	DATE	COLOUR	AWARDS	HEIGHT
1	Joffre	1931	yellow	AM H 31	10in/25cm
1	Bellona	1944	gold		12in/30cm
2	Baby Doll	1961	buttercup-yellow		8in/20cm
3	Golden Show	1944	deep gold		20in/50cm
4	Golden Oxford	1959	pure golden-yellow	HC W 78	24in/60cm
4	Jewel of Spring	1956	sulphur-yellow	AM H 60. FCC W 78	24in/60cm
4	Olympic Gold	1962	buttercup-yellow		22in/55cm
5	Golden Harvest	c1922	lemon-yellow	AM H 28	26in/65cm
5	Bingham	1950	gold	AM H 50	25in/62.5cm
5	Inglescombe yellow	c1901	yellow	AM H 14, AM W 06	22in/55cm
5	Mrs John T Scheepers	1930	canary-yellow	FCC H 31	24in/60cm
6	West Point	1943	bright lemon	HC W 82	20in/50cm
6	Golden Duchess	1938	deep primrose-yellow	FCC H 39	20in/50cm
7	Maja	1968	Dresden yellow		26in/65cm
7	Fringed Elegance	1974	sulphur-yellow	AM H 74	24in/60cm
10	Texas Gold	1944	clear yellow		21in/52.5cm
11	Gold Medal	1946	deep yellow		18in/45cm
11	Ostara	1958	lemon	AM H 60	20in/50cm
12	Berlioz	1942	gold/red blotched	AM W 39	8in/20cm
13	Yellow Purissima	1980	barium yellow		20in/50cm
13	Candela	1961	pure yellow	AM H 61	20in/50cm
15	*uremiensis*	1932	clear yellow	FCC W 70	5in/12.5cm
15	*batalinii*		lemon-yellow	AM H 00. FCC W 70	5in/12.5cm

Three fascinating tulips which have been in this section for many years are 'Temple of Beauty' and its two sports. 'Temple of Beauty' was introduced in 1959 by D. W. Lefeber and Co. Mr Lefeber himself stated that the parentage was lily-flowering 'Mariette' crossed with greigii. It was classified as a greigii hybrid until 1963, but in 1969 it was transferred to the cottage class, although the classified list itself stated that it had an enormous lily-shaped flower and the leaves were slightly mottled. 'Temple of Beauty' is a salmon rose orange colour throughout. One of its sports, 'Blushing Beauty', is a soft orange pink fading into yellow orange toward the edges of the petal. On the other, 'Hocus Pocus', the three outer petals are almost pure buttercup yellow, while the inner three are coloured scarlet red.

Special mention must be made of the tetraploid, 'Mrs John T. Scheepers', a light canary yellow with very large flowers and pointed petals. It has often been described as the best yellow tulip ever raised. It has a deep yellow sport called 'Gold Rush'.

Two cultivars in this section date back to 1630. The first is 'Gala Beauty', with synonyms 'Columbus' and 'French Crown'. It is yellow flamed carmine. The other is 'Zomerschoon', which is salmon rose on cream. 'Zomerschoon' is very expensive and I am not sure if 'Gala Beauty' is still obtainable.

DOUBLE LATE TULIPS

Double late tulips are often called peony-flowering tulips. The history is somewhat murky but it is known that most of the early varieties had very weak necks and the flower heads tended to hang because of their weight.

'Blue Flag (Bleu Celeste)' was raised in 1750. It is a light violet and may still be obtainable, but almost all the other cultivars now on sale have been raised since 1932. 'Lilac Perfection' is an excellent lilac and one of the best in this section. 'Clara Carder' is tyrian purple and 'Maravilla' is a rich violet. 'Gerbrandt Kieft' is a glowing purple red edged white, while 'Hermione' is a light violet rose.

'Gold Medal' is a deep yellow and 'Ostara' is lemon, being a sport of 'Golden Harvest'. 'Mount Tacoma' is probably the best of the whites.

Some of the most popular members of this section are bi-colours. 'Coxa' is carmine vermilion edged white. It has a sport, 'Orange Triumph' which is orange red flushed brown with a narrow yellow edge. Also very popular is 'Nizza', which is yellow with red stripes. Of its sports, 'Golden Nizza' is gold feathered red and 'Carnaval de Nice' is white with red stripes. 'Bonanza' is carmine red edged yellow, and 'Allegretto' and 'Amusement' are also red edged yellow.

'Uncle Tom' is maroon red and 'Eros' is old rose. 'Symphonia' is a cherry rose and is a sport of 'Pride of Haarlem'. 'May Wonder' is also rose. 'Granda' is carmine rose but it has produced a sport, 'Angelique', which is one of the most beautiful in this section. It is a pale pink with a lighter edge and is extremely popular at present although it has been in cultivation for over 30 years.

MOUNT TACOMA	
Classification	Double late (peony flowered)
Year introduced	1926
Height	22in/55cm
Awards	FCC H 39

ALLEGRETTO	
Classification	Double late
Year introduced	1963
Height	14in/35cm

LILAC PERFECTION

Classification	Double late (peony flowered)
Year introduced	1951
Height	18in/45cm

UNCLE TOM

Classification	Double late (peony flowered)
Height	20in/50cm
Awards	AM H 39

MAY WONDER

Classification	Double late
Year introduced	1951
Height	16in/40cm

ANGELIQUE

Classification	Double late (peony flowered)
Year introduced	1959
Height	16in/40cm

A Rembrandt in a group of late singles.
~

REMBRANDT AND FLORISTS TULIPS

Many will suggest that the tulips in this chapter are now obsolete but they are still popular with a good number of people who would disagree with that view.

All these tulips are 'broken' or 'rectified', which means that the flower's anthocyanin pigment, which had been diffused over the whole petal, gathers in certain restricted areas. Stripes and splashes are the result, with the ground between white or yellow and no longer modified by the anthocyanin. This breaking we now know is caused by TBV (tulip breaking virus) and is transmitted from one plant to another mostly by aphis but possibly by other forms of life.

These broken tulips became known as florists tulips in the seventeenth century, when the effects were first noticed. They were divided into six classes. Roses had white grounds with pink to crimson scarlet markings. Bijbloemens had white grounds with purple markings and Bizarres had yellow grounds with red and brown markings. Each colour group had two classes, feathered and flamed. The markings of a feathered flower are confined to the edges of the petal. The edges should be continuous and finely pencilled but the depth may vary considerably with the variety. In some the edge forms a thin picotte, but never a wire edge. In others it is deeply laid and may extend a quarter of the way down the petal. It will always run more deeply down the centre of the petal, forming what is called a beard. The colour, however fine and pencilled, should be quite definite and uniform; the rest of the flower beyond the feathering on the edge should be pure white or yellow. In a flamed flower, in addition to the feathering just described, there should be a beam of colour up the centre of the petal, branching as it ascends and merging with the feathering at the edge. This beam should be symmetrical and the branching should be fine, without any broad stripes running out to the edge of the petal. The colouring should be dense and well defined against the white or yellow ground, though as a rule, if the beam is broad, it will show some lighter colour in the middle.

These broken tulips of various forms had their own classification until 1969, when they were all amalgamated into one section and given the name of Rembrandt tulips.

Group		Group	
BROKEN TULIPS			
NOT CAUSED BY VIRUS			
1	'Mickey Mouse'	6	'Marylyn'
1	'Montparnasse'	10	'Estella Rijveld'
1	'Prince Carnival'	10	'Flaming Parrot'
4	'Dutch Fair'	11	'Carnaval de Nice'
4	'Flaming Gold'	11	'Nizza'
4	'Olympic Flame'	11	'Texas Flame'
5	'American Flag'		
5	'Cordell Hull'		
5	'San Marino'		
5	'Sorbet'		
5	'Union Jack'		

For about three centuries florists tulips were the dominating force in all tulip growing. When it was learnt early on that aphis would enable tulips to break, growers encouraged aphis on their tulip beds. In these earlier centuries nothing was known about virus diseases. In the early years of this century virus was realized as a possible source of infection. Although experiments were carried out at the John Innes Horticultural Institute in the late 1920s by Dr E. J. Collins and Miss D. M. Caley, it was not until 1932 that the existence of virus was considered proven.

In England, Holland, Flanders and northern France many societies and associations were set up to promote the growth, exchange and sale of florists tulips. Many of these organizations ceased to exist as soon as they realized that the flowers they loved were diseased.

Capsules with aphis.

Some of these broken tulips can be beautiful and for centuries they have provided inspiration for Dutch, Flemish and English painters. Tulips have been painted by Hans Bollongier, Jan van Os, Maria S. Merian, Jan Brueghel II, J. Marrel, H. Henstenburgh, H. G. Knip, Alexander Marshal, Otto Marcellis, and perhaps above all Judith Leyster a Haarlem artist, who was both niece and pupil to Frans Hals. She even produced a complete book of illustrations of broken tulips.

When I first grew Rembrandt tulips, I had never heard of tulip breaking virus. However, I soon discovered that many of my other tulips were soon infected by the virus with consequence of heavy losses. In an eighteenth-century tulip book, the horticulturalist D. H. Cause stated that a poor bulb produces a flower more beautiful than before and shortly afterwards dies, as if it has used its last strength to please its owner. The beauty of such

A Rembrandt tulip.

~

flowers is a beauty of death. The prettier a flower, the closer it was to dying.

Not many professional tulip growers grow broken tulips any more. If they do they try to isolate them well away from all other varieties. The minimum distance is stated to be 80 ft (about 25 m). Presumably this is farther than aphis will fly. In the latest classified list (1987) the Royal General Dutch Bulb Growers' Association (KAVB) stated that there were so few Rembrandt tulips now being grown that the classification would cease. They have, however, now told me that the classification Rembrandts will not be replaced because of its historical importance.

Broken tulips have certainly played their part in the popularity of the tulip. Tulips have survived and now their popularity is due to much more solid reasons.

I recognize the beauty of broken tulips but at the same time am always reminded of death, so I try to kill every aphis in my garden and I burn any plants affected by TBV.

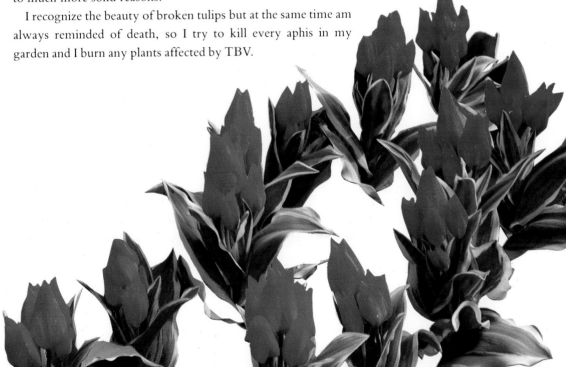

Picotee
~

OTHER LATE TULIPS
LILY-FLOWERED, FRINGED, VIRIDIFLORA AND PARROT TULIPS

Until recently lily-flowered, fringed and viridiflora tulips were all part of the cottage class, which was a convenient gathering ground for several tulips which could not be placed elsewhere. The cottage class included a number of pseudospecies, such as retroflexa, viridiflora and acuminata. The lily-flowered tulips were given their own classification space in 1958 and the viridiflora and fringed tulips were given separate space from 1981.

LILY-FLOWERED TULIPS

Retroflexa (primrose) and elegans alba (white with a rose edge) are still in the classified list. Elegans alba appears to have been replaced at the beginning of the century by 'Picotee', and that in turn now seems to be replaced by 'Elegant Lady', which is cream yellow edged violet red.

The lily shape of these flowers is clearly more important than their size which is well adapted to those who enjoy flower arranging. Nevertheless, one of my favourites in this section, 'Mariette',

MARIETTE	
Classification	Lily-flowered
Year introduced	1942
Height	23in/57.5cm
Awards	FCC H 50 AM W 68

is probably the largest. It is a deep satin rose with a white base. Its sport, 'Marjolein', is orange and carmine rose with pepper red inside. Other good pinks are 'China Pink' (uniform satin pink) and 'Jacqueline' (deep rose). 'Gisella' (sometimes called 'Giselle') is a good pink and 'Astor' is an excellent salmon pink.

'Maytime' is a purple violet and 'Lilac Time' is a violet purple. 'Burgundy' is a deep purplish violet and 'Linette' is also purple. 'Captain Fryatt' is ruby purple and 'Ballade' is violet mauve with a white edge. 'Dyanito' is a glowing red of good tone and 'Aladdin' is clear crimson with a yellow edge. 'Queen of Sheba' is a brownish red edged yellow and 'Stanislaus' is red edged yellow. 'Red Shine' is a violet carmine. 'Hedwig Vatter' is orange, 'Golden Duchess' is a primrose yellow and 'West Point' is a bright lemon. Needless to say, 'White Triumphator' is white.

MAYTIME	
Classification	Lily-flowered
Year introduced	1942
Height	19in/47.5cm

MARJOLEIN	
Classification	Lily-flowered
Year introduced	1962
Height	23in/57.5cm
Awards	AM W 82

CHINA PINK	
Classification	Lily-flowered
Year introduced	1944
Height	20in/50cm

BURGUNDY	
Classification	Lily-flowered
Year introduced	1957
Height	19in/47.5cm

BALLADE	
Year introduced	1953
Height	19in/47.5cm

ALADDIN	
Classification	Lily-flowered
Year introduced	1942
Height	20in/50cm

QUEEN OF SHEBA	
Classification	Lily-flowered
Year introduced	1944
Height	19in/47.5cm
Awards	AM W 68

RED SHINE	
Classification	Lily-flowering
Year introduced	1955
Height	25in/62.5cm

WHITE TRIMPHATOR	
Classification	Lily-flowered
Year introduced	1942
Height	28in/70cm
Awards	HC W 82

FRINGED TULIPS

Until 1981 these were included mostly in the cottage and Darwin class and there were not many of them. The first to appear was 'Sundew', a sport of the red Darwin 'Orion'. Then came 'The Skipper', a sport of a breeder tulip, 'Louis XIV'. Two early sports followed: 'Arma', sport of 'Couleur Cardinal', and 'Fringed Beauty', sport of the double early 'Titian'. These two remain the only early fringed tulips and they are of course both dwarf. For quite a time it was believed that fringed tulips only came from sports, as did the parrot tulips, but in the early 1950s a number of seedlings appeared.

Those first seedlings were not particularly successful. Then, between 1959 and 1975, more than 30 fringed tulips were raised and introduced by Segers Brothers. Many of these form the basis of the collection of fringed-tulips now on sale and a good number are beautiful. (Unfortunately, after making such a magnificent contribution to the beauty of the tulip, Segers Brothers went out of business in 1975.) 'Swan Wings' was the first to be introduced, a pure white which arrived in 1959. The vigorous 'Burgundy Lace' (1961) is wine red with a crystalline fringe; for most of its life it has been one of the cheapest in this section. After 'Burgundy Lace', two other good reds are 'Hellas' and 'Red Wing'. 'Noranda' is a deep blood red tinted orange at the edges and 'Aleppo' is a dull spyrea red with an apricot-coloured fringe and an apricot-coloured centre.

BELLE FLOWER	
Classification	Fringed
Year introduced	1970
Height	20in/50cm

In my experience one of the most robust of the fringed tulips is 'Maja', which ranges from Dresden yellow to mimosa yellow. Another good yellow is 'Laverock', which is barium yellow outside and canary yellow in. Two good pinks are 'Belle Flower' (rose bengal outside and cherry red inside) and 'Burns' (phlox pink). Two excellent purples are 'Blue Heron' (violet purple) and 'Canova' (cobalt violet tinted purple).

A popular new variety is 'Fancy Frills'. Its exterior is ivory white and the top and side of the petals are edged with rose Bengal with a crystalline white rose coloured fringe. My favourite is 'Johann Gutenberg'. The colour of this tulip is difficult to describe, indeed every catalogue that I have seen describes it differently. The official colour is Indian lake tinted red, but I think a better description is deep carmine pink with primrose fringes and a buff blush over the entire bloom.

In addition to these new seedlings from Segers Brothers there have also been three sports of Darwin hybrid tulips. 'Fringed Apeldoorn' and 'Fringed Golden Apeldoorn' speak for themselves. 'Fringed Elegance' is a sport of 'Jewel of Spring'. The three of them have the same colouring, habit of growth and durability of their parents. They will grow in similar conditions if required. Because of their relatively recent introduction and high demand, the fringed tulips mentioned are slightly expensive. Things should soon settle down, and it is certainly worth trying some of them.

BURGUNDY LACE	
Classification	Fringed
Year introduced	1961
Height	26in/65cm
Awards	AM W 70

FANCY FRILLS	
Classification	Fringed
Year introduced	1972
Height	20in/50cm

FRINGED ELEGANCE	
Classification	Fringed
Year introduced	1974
Height	24in/60cm
Awards	AM H 74

VIRIDIFLORA TULIPS

Until 1981 these were all treated as cottage tulips or single lates. *Tulipa viridiflora* (yellow and green) is one of the pseudospecies which have never been seen in the wild. It has been in cultivation since 1700. 'Viridiflora praecox' is larger, more early flowering and is a pale yellow and green. It is not too vigorous and therefore rather expensive. One of the first hybrids was 'Formosa' (yellow and green), which won the Award of Merit in 1926. Then came 'Greenland' (green and rose) and 'Pimpernel' (purple red and green). They received the Award of Merit in 1960 and 1961 respectively. Meanwhile, 1947 saw the introduction of a dwarf variety called 'Artist'. Inside 'Artist' is salmon rose and green, outside it is purple and salmon rose. It grows to a height of about 11 in (28 cm). It has a number of interesting sports. 'Golden Artist' is golden orange with green stripes and 'Hollywood' is red tinged green. 'Esperanto' is itself a sport of 'Hollywood' and it is china rose with a green midrib fading into red brown. It also has variegated leaves with a silvery white edge to the green leaves.

GREENLAND	
Classification	Viridiflora
Year introduced	1955
Height	20in/50cm
Awards	AM H 60

Other excellent viridiflora tulips are 'Hummingbird', which has a square head on a sturdy stem and a wide blaze of orchid green and orchid yellow at the edges, and 'Florosa' with a white outer base fading to a broad pink edge and a long green yellow flame. 'Court Lady' is green and white and 'Doll's Minuet' is glowing tyrian purple with green. 'Cherie' is deep yellow and green and 'Grasshopper' is white, creamy yellow and green. 'Dancing Show' is canary yellow and green and 'Green Spot' is white with green stripes. 'Green Eyes' is green yellow with spinach green and 'Groene Ridder' (sometimes referred to as 'Green Knight') is yellow and green. Of the newer varieties, the cheapest and probably the most vigorous is 'Spring Green' with a neat head of orchid green with a broad white edge and within shading to orchid yellow to ivory white at the tips.

These viridiflora tulips do make a good show in the border but they are probably used mostly for flower arranging.

ARTIST	
Classification	Viridiflora
Year introduced	1947
Height	16in/40cm
Awards	AM H 47

COURT LADY	
Classification	Viridiflora
Year introduced	1956
Height	16in/40cm

SPRING GREEN	
Classification	Viridiflora
Year introduced	1969
Height	16in/40cm

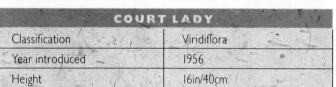

Recommended Tulips
(including Bi-colours)

CLASSIFICATION GROUP	NAME	DATE	COLOUR	AWARDS	HEIGHT
1	Beauty Queen	1979	rose/salmon		16in/40cm
1	Keizerskroon	1750	red/yellow		14in/35cm
3	Abu Hassan	1976	mahogany/yellow		20in/50cm
3	Alela	1980	ivory/rose		18in/45cm
3	Annie Schilder	1982	pink/orange		20in/50cm
3	Happy Family	1985	purple/rose		18in/45cm
3	Valentine	1970	rose-purple/white		20in/50cm
4	Daydream	1980	marigold-orange		24in/60cm
4	Oxford's Elite	1968	orange-red yellow		24in/60cm
4	Queen Wilhelmina	1965	red/orange/yellow	FCC W 69	22in/55cm
5	Blushing Beauty	1983	red/yellow		26in/65cm
5	Georgette	1952	yellow-red		20in/50cm
5	Magier	1951	white/violet-blue		26in/65cm
5	Menton	1971	rose/red/orange		25in/62.5cm
5	Pandion	c.1950	purple/white	FCC H 54. AM W 57	24in/60cm
5	Rose van Lima	1943	lilac-rose/salmon		20in/50cm
5	Temple of Beauty	1959	salmon-rose		26in/65cm
6	Aladdin	1942	scarlet-yellow		20in/50cm

Recommended Tulips (including Bi-colours)

CLASSIFICATION GROUP	NAME	DATE	COLOUR	AWARDS	HEIGHT
6	Elegant Lady	1953	cream/violet-red		20in/50cm
6	Queen of Sheba	1944	brownish-red/orange	AM W 68	19in/47.5cm
7	Aleppo	1969	red/apricot		21in/52.5cm
7	Fancy Frills	1972	white/rose		20in/50cm
7	Noranda	1971	red/orange		21in/52.5cm
8	Esperanto	1968	green/rose/silver		12in/30cm
8	Greenland	1955	green/rose/cream	AM H 60	20in/50cm
8	Spring Green	1969	green/ivory/yellow		16in/40cm
10	Rococo	1942	carmine/scarlet	AM H 44	12in/30cm
11	Bonanza	1943	carmine/yellow	AM H 43	16in/40cm
11	Nizza	1939	yellow/red	FCC H.49	20in/50cm
12	Ancilla	1955	red/white/pink		8in/20cm
12	Cesar Franck	1940	carmine/yellow		12in/30cm
12	Corona	c.1943	red/yellow	AM W 48	10in/25cm
12	The First	1940	carmine/ivory		10in/25cm
12	Franz Lehar	1955	sulphur/red		7in/17.5cm
13	Ballet	1952	red/white/pink		10in/25cm
13	Dance	1952	red/white/pink	AM W 54	10in/25cm
13	Grand Prix	1949	scarlet/yellow	AM H 49	18in/45cm
13	Rondo	1952	vermilion/gold		16in/40cm
13	Salut	1955	carmine/sulphur		10in/25cm
14	Cape Cod	1955	apricot/yellow		15in/37.5cm
14	Plaisir	1953	carmine/sulphur		9in/22.5cm
14	Treasure	1963	tangerine/orange		8in/20cm
14	Yellow Dawn	1953	old rose/indian yellow	HC W 66	9in/22.5cm
15	*hageri* splendens	1945	coppery-bronze		8in/20cm
15	*praestans* Unicum	1975	capsicum-red		12in/30cm
15	*tarda*		white/brown	AM H 37. AM W 70	4in/10cm

PARROT TULIPS

Unlike the other groups in this chapter, the parrot tulips have always had their own section. In addition, although placed in this chapter, they are by no means all late tulips. They are all sports of other varieties. Little is known of their origin, although it has been known for over three centuries that they cannot be reproduced by seed. 'Amiral de Constantinople' and 'lutea major' both date from 1665; 'Perfecta' and 'Markgraaf' date from 1750. One theory as to their origin suggests that they are induced by some virus, but experimental evidence is not forthcoming to back this up. Unlike the other groups in this chapter, not all Parrots are late blooming. One of the best-known varieties, 'Karel Doorman', is a sport of the Triumph tulip 'Alberio'. 'Doorman' itself has many sports and there are other sports of Mendel and Triumph tulips.

FANTASY	
Classification	Parrot
Year introduced	1910
Height	22in/55cm
Awards	FCC H 22 AM W 21

BLUE PARROT	
Classification	Parrot
Year introduced	1935
Height	24in/60cm
Awards	A.M.H 35

There are five sports of single early tulips. 'Rex' is a sport of 'Keizerskroon', 'Rococo' is a sport of 'Couleur Cardinal', 'Gemma' is a sport of 'La Reine', 'Henrik Ibsen' is a sport of 'Pluvia d'Oro' and 'Rosy Parrot' a sport of 'Ibis'. There are also three sports of double early tulips. 'Parrot Blossom' is a sport of 'Peach Blossom', 'Rosy Cloud' a sport of 'Murillo' and 'Vesuvius' is a sport of 'Scarlet Cardinal'. In the early days most of the parrot tulips hung their heads and they were not popular. In any case there were not that many of them. A major change took place in 1910, when 'Fantasy' was introduced. This is a sport of 'Clara Butt' and has the same salmon pink colour, though with green stripes. It is very large and held on a good stem, and has three sports of its own. Most of the parrot tulips have much the same colour as the tulip that they sported from, though often with a few green stripes. 'Blue Parrot' is a sport of 'Bleu Aimable' and 'Black Parrot' is a sport of 'Phillipe de Comines'. 'Apricot Parrot', 'Salmon Parrot' and 'Vermilion Parrot' are all sports of 'Karel Doorman'. 'Orange Parrot' a sport of 'Orange Beauty', 'Red Parrot' a sport of 'Gloria Swanson'; 'White Parrot' is a sport of 'Albino' and 'Yellow Parrot' is a sport of 'Golden Harvest'.

ESTELLA RIJNVELD	
Classification	Parrot
Year introduced	1954
Height	24in/60cm

TEXAS GOLD	
Classification	Parrot
Year introduced	1944
Height	21in/52.5cm

Other interesting varieties are 'Estella Rijnveld', sport of 'Red Champion'. It has waved petals of white richly marked raspberry red. 'Flaming Parrot' is a sport of 'Red Parrot' which is creamy yellow flamed and feathered rosy red. 'Orange Favourite' is a uniform orange scarlet tinged old rose with featherings of apple green. It is a sport of 'Orange King'. 'Red Champion' (glistening red) is a sport of 'Bartigon'. 'Texas Gold', a sport of 'Inglescombe Yellow', is clear yellow with a narrow red ribbon round the edges of the petals. This itself has three more sports, 'Texas Cocktail', 'Texas Fire' and 'Texas Flame', which is a bright buttercup yellow flamed carmine red. 'Bird of Paradise', a sport of 'Bandoeng', is a very interesting variety being cardinal red edged orange with a bright yellow base and a strong grower.

FLAMING PARROT	
Classification	Parrot
Year introduced	1968
Height	24in/60cm

Spring Pearl
~

BOTANICAL TULIPS

These days the botanical tulips are the true early ones, coming into bloom from March onwards. Sometimes they are as early as February and in a special year even January. They brighten up the spring and give great joy. Botanical tulips have become very popular recently. Although a few have been available for about 50 years, they have only now come down in price to a point where every gardener can afford them.

They bloom early and the foliage dies down early so they can be lifted earlier than most tulips. This gives ample opportunity for planting the summer bedding. If they are grown in separate beds from the mid-season and later tulips, then the lifting and summer bedding can be done in series. This provides plenty of opportunity for different kinds of summer bedding if so desired.

All the varieties or cultivars mentioned in this chapter are robust and the great majority are extremely vigorous. As a result most of them are now much cheaper than many of the older tulips. The three botanical species mentioned in this chapter are the kaufmanniana, greigii and fosteriana tulips, all of which arrived in the West from Central Asia, mostly Turkestan. With the exception of the fosteriana the original species have been very largely overtaken and replaced by some of the more robust and vigorous hybrids. From the three the interbreeding has been very considerable and has produced a remarkable race of new tulips.

KAUFMANNIANA

The original kaufmanniana species tulip is still grown. It remains very vigorous and cheap, but it does tend to be knocked over by the wind. It has largely been replaced by some of the larger hybrids such as 'The First' and 'Elliott'. 'The First' is, logically, usually the first to bloom. It is brighter and larger than the species and is just as vigorous. It has a long red and white flower of considerable vigour.

Most tulips open in the sun but close again at night. Kaufmannianas open especially wide and are often described as a water lily tulip. Quite often, the open centre of the flower is more beautiful than the outside. I do not think this applies to 'The First', with its long slender red and white exterior.

Next to bloom is 'Early Harvest', one of my favourites. This is one of three Rijnveld introductions from 1966. In 1973 it became the only kaufmanniana in recent years to win the Award of Merit Hillegom. 'Early Harvest' is certainly the most free-flowering of the 760 tulip varieties that I have grown. It gives many offsets. Most of these will flower after only one year. It is a reddish orange tulip with a yellow edge and the inside is orange flamed on yellow.

Kaufmannianas Early Harvest and Showwinner.

LOVE SONG	
Classification	Kaufmanniana
Year introduced	1966
Height	8in/20cm

THE FIRST	
Classification	Kaufmanniana
Year introduced	1940
Height	10in/25cm

Its sister seedling, 'Love Song', blooms about five days later. At first glance it resembles 'Early Harvest', but the exterior is somewhat redder and the yellow edge narrower. They are even more similar when fully open in the sun. The bases of the anthers of 'Love Song' are violet, the foliage is greyish and the stem immediately below the bloom is greener.

The third cultivar from the Rijnveld stable in 1966 is the bright scarlet 'Showwinner'. By far the best of the early reds, it is also a vigorous and robust tulip.

Three pinks must now be mentioned – 'Fritz Kreisler', 'Jeantine' and 'Duplosa'. Just before, during and shortly after the Second World War, the firm of van Tubergen introduced a large range of kaufmannianas crossed with both fosteriana and greigii tulips. Arguably 'Fritz Kreisler' is the most beautiful. It is a pale salmon pink lightly tinged mauve with a narrow cream edge. The centre is yellow blotched with carmine. It is taller than most and a large flower with clear indications of fosteriana blood. 'Fritz Kreisler' does not produce many offsets and is consequently still somewhat more expensive than its companions.

CESAR FRANCK	
Classification	Kaufmanniana
Year introduced	1940
Height	12in/30cm

DUPLOSA	
Classification	Kaufmanniana
Year introduced	1955
Height	9in/22.5cm

'Jeantine', another van Tubergen pink, is slightly smaller and comes in carmine pink with a lighter edge and gold centre. It is extremely vigorous and should be very cheap. After 'Early Harvest' it is probably the most free-flowering of the kaufmanniana hybrids. Very different and extremely attractive is 'Duplosa', a unique semi-double in raspberry pink with a gold centre. It is sometimes the first to bloom in the garden.

There are several good red and yellow bi-colours in the kaufmanniana section. 'Cesar Franck' is usually the earliest. It is carmine red and gold and has green leaves. 'Cesar Franck' comes from the Rijnveld firm; the others come from van Tubergen. The relatively cheap 'Stresa' is currant red and Indian yellow. It is sometimes described as harsh or even garish but it is certainly popular. Probably the most perfect bloom in this group is 'Goudstuk'. It is deep carmine and gold and is one of van Tubergen's best. It is also a little shy in producing offsets, so although not as expensive as 'Fritz Kreisler' it is a little more than most. 'Solanus' flowers a good deal later and resembles a fosteriana. 'Corona' is red and pale yellow; its centre is gold with a broad scarlet band. 'Corona' certainly has the best centre in the kaufmanniana section, apart from 'Joseph Kafka'. Van Tubergen once described 'Joseph Kafka' as their best hybrid but it now appears to be off the market.

CORONA	
Classification	Kaufmanniana
Year introduced	c1943
Height	10in/25cm
Awards	AM W 48

BERLIOZ	
Classification	Kaufmanniana
Year introduced	1942
Height	8in/20cm
Awards	AM W 39

Crossbreeding has given many kaufmannianas and a few fosterianas the striped and mottled foliage of the greigiis. Possibly the most attractive foliage of the kaufmannianas belongs to 'Franz Lehar'. The leaves are very blue with purple stripes. Unfortunately the blooms in pink and white are somewhat colourless. Two later dwarf cultivars 'flower off' pink, meaning they open red and white and gradually become suffused with pink as the bloom matures. 'Heart's Delight' has good foliage and is vigorous and very popular. 'Ancilla' has a good centre and is also very popular. It will grow well indoors. Several other cultivars in other sections flower off in this way. Notable among the fosterianas are 'Dance', 'Zombie', 'Ballet', 'Mitella' and 'Honorose'. The greigii 'Roseanna' and 'Mary Ann' also flower off. 'Scarlet Baby' and 'Berlioz' are noteworthy among the later blooming kaufmannianas. 'Scarlet Baby', with bright green leaves and a good yellow centre, is very reliable and vigorous. 'Berlioz' is very bright and cheerful. Although it has red blotches on the outside it is sometimes described as being all-gold and certainly gives that appearance when fully open in the sun.

FOSTERIANAS

When the fosteriana tulips were first brought from central Asia into western Europe they were stated to be rather variable. Various clones were selected from these imports. 'Princeps' is stated in the classified list to be so selected, but many people believe that another selection was the best-known fosteriana of all – 'Madame Lefeber' or 'Red Emperor'. It is certainly the seed parent of a large number of the hybrids. A large tulip about 10 in (25 cm) across, it is a fiery oriental red with a black yellow edged centre. It has often been described as the most beautiful of all tulips. In a good year it will give a magnificent performance. Its stem is somewhat less than perfect and the combination of heavy rain followed by very strong winds can do great damage.

This weakness also affects some of the taller hybrids bred from 'Madame Lefeber'. These include 'Spring Pearl', which is pearl grey edged deep pink and inside pink with a yellow base. 'Solva' is similar but without any pearl grey on the exterior. These two are raised by Rijnveld. 'Sylvia van Lennep' is a similar pink but has a black yellow edged base. 'Easter Parade' and its sport 'Hi Parade' are both red edged yellow with yellow inside. 'Zombie' is red and white with yellow inside with a base of black edged red. It flowers-off pink and is one of a considerable group of Fosterianas raised in the early 1950s by C. V. Hybrida to flower off pink.

These seven tulips are all beautiful and worth growing. Because of the slight stem weakness they should be planted in smaller groups or possibly surrounded by varieties with stronger stems. Fortunately, the extreme rain and wind is rare in most areas. Of those with stronger stems 'Orange Emperor' is outstanding. It is a carrot orange with a buttercup centre and a rigid stem, one of the very best and can be grown virtually anywhere. I have grown a large block of 340 of these tulips in my main bed and they have given an excellent show for many years now.

SPRING PEARL	
Classification	Fosteriana
Year introduced	1955
Height	18in/45cm

ORANGE EMPEROR	
Classification	Fosteriana
Year introduced	1962
Height	20in/50cm

SWEETHEART	
Classification	Fosteriana
Year introduced	1976
Height	15in/37.5cm

PURISSIMA	
Classification	Fosteriana
Year introduced	1943
Height	20in/50cm
Awards	AM·H 49

Another excellent cultivar is 'Orange Brilliant', which is slightly brighter and possibly a bit less vigorous. The official colour is a bright indian orange with a yellow base. Another outstanding tall tulip with an excellent stem is van Tubergen's 'Purissima', often described as the best white tulip ever raised. Sometimes called 'White Emperor', it is a milky white with a yellow centre. 'Purissima's' excellent shape and stature help it stand up to almost any weather. More recently two sports have been developed from this variety. The first was 'Sweetheart', with barium yellow towards the bottom of the bloom and ivory white at the top. It is an attractive tulip and has become very popular since it was introduced in 1976. Four years later 'Yellow Purissima' was introduced. It is a barium yellow tulip with a bright canary yellow edge. The centre is also bright yellow. Although I have only been growing 'Yellow Purissima' for one year, I feel confident that it will be comfortably the most popular of all the yellows of this group.

CANTATA	
Classification	Fosteriana
Height	11in/27.5cm
Awards	AM H 42

SALUT	
Classification	Fosteriana
Year introduced	1955
Height	10in/25cm

Previously, the best of the taller yellows was probably 'Candela', though there are several others which could claim this title. Of the taller reds, 'Galata' is excellent. It grows well and vigorously. 'Pinkeen', from van Tubergen, opens cerise pink but flowers-off to a deeper rose-red with a yellow centre. It is usually the earliest of the fosterianas to flower. I have known it to be in bloom in the open garden on 10 January.

There are also many shorter-stemmed fosterianas which are highly recommendable. 'Princeps' is a scarlet clone taken from the wild species. Despite its name it is not early, but it is a good grower and is a very bright red. 'Rockery Beauty' is blood red and even dwarfer in stature and even later in flowering. But of this group the best is probably 'Cantata'. It is a vivid orange scarlet with a faint buff flush up the middle of the petals, which bloom above glossy apple-green foliage.

Next come six more of the C.V. Hybrida group. They are all much shorter than 'Zombie'. The first four all flower-off pink. The best of the bunch is undoubtedly 'Dance', which has the most beautiful centre of all the botanical tulips. It is black with a broad and growing band of brilliant scarlet with golden stamens. As the petals flower-off pink it remains extremely beautiful. 'Ballet', 'Mitella' and 'Honorose' also flower-off pink. They are all similar to 'Dance' on the exterior but do not have its perfect centre. 'Concerto' is sulphur white outside and in with a black yellow edged base. 'Salut' is similar but it has a carmine pink edged sulphur white exterior and is probably more robust and vigorous. It is very easy to grow.

In the fosteriana section there are three excellent red and yellow bi-colours. 'Reginald Dixon' is scarlet edged gold, inside lemon with a black base with red blotches. It grows best in a heavy soil and tends to be expensive. 'Rondo' and van Tubergen's 'Grand Prix' are similar in colour but both have a golden centre blotched red. 'Grand Prix' in particular is an excellent tulip for naturalizing and will grow virtually anywhere.

Crossbreeding has brought a number of fosterianas with greigii leaves. Six of these were introduced by van Tubergen in 1961. Two of the six – 'Toulon' and 'Juan' – are still on sale. 'Toulon' is probably better, being slightly shorter and with good stems. It is a vivid deep orange tulip with a centre that is a deep brown edged yellow with pale yellow anthers. The leaves are beautifully striped a reddish brown. 'Juan' has extremely similar foliage but is slightly taller and in certain circumstances the stems are not quite perfect. It is a slightly paler orange than 'Toulon' and has an unusually large yellow base.

RONDO	
Classification	Fosteriana
Year introduced	1952
Height	16in/40cm

TOULON	
Classification	Fosteriana
Year introduced	1961
Height	15in/37.5cm
Awards	HC W 66

JUAN	
Classification	Fosteriana
Year introduced	1961
Height	16in/40cm

GREIGII

The greigii species tulips actually arrived in western Europe before the kaufmanniana. The basic species is a bright orange scarlet with vivid striped and patterned leaves. The stripes sometimes look purple and sometimes brown. There are two variations. 'Greigii Aurea' has yellow and red. 'Greigii Alba' has white and red. Although greigii is robust it does not produce very many offsets. It was not highly regarded until the spate of crossbreeding between greigii, kaufmanniana and fosteriana began about 40 years ago. The latest classified list contains over 220 greigii tulips, so only a few can be described here. Some of them do not appear to be happy in extremely heavy soil. This may be because slugs, which will attack almost any tulip, do seem to find the greigii bulbs and their foliage particularly appetizing.

An outstanding exception is the variety 'Toronto'. It is very vigorous in any soil and an extremely good bulb maker. 'Toronto' is a self-coloured coral pink with a yellow base with brownish blotches. It is also multi-flowering, branch flowering or bunch flowering. A number of tulipas such as 'Jeantine', 'Grand Prix', 'Galata', 'Salut', 'Concerto' and 'Compostella' throw up secondary blooms, but 'Toronto' is a genuine multi-flora. It has recently shown a tendency to throw sports; I have a red 'Toronto', but with only one bulb it is certainly not yet established. One called 'Orange Toronto' is now on sale. It has only just arrived and I have not seen it grown, but if it corresponds to description it should fill a useful gap in this section.

There are a number of attractive orange greigii but they do not appear to be especially robust and they all seem to have gone off the market. 'Orange 'Elite' is possibly the best. It is rose edged orange outside and a pure orange inside. 'Compostella' is orange flamed on yellow while 'Rockery Wonder' is orange with a bronze flush. 'Toronto' is certainly the best of the pinks but there are other good ones. 'Perlina' is a porcelain rose colour with a yellow base. 'Salmon Joy' is salmon rose edged primrose outside and azalea rose edged white inside. 'Sweet Lady' is peach-blossom and 'Dreamboat' is yellow flamed red giving a pink effect. 'Oratorio' is apricot rose and a black base and has extremely attractive foliage.

TORONTO	
Classification	Greigii
Year introduced	1963
Height	12in/30cm

DREAMBOAT	
Classification	Greigii
Year introduced	1953
Height	10in/25cm
Awards	AM W 66

ORATORIO	
Classification	Greigii
Year introduced	1952
Height	7in/17.5cm
Awards	HC W 66

DONNA BELLA	
Classification	Greigii
Year introduced	1955
Height	8in/20cm

ROSEANNA	
Classification	Greigii
Year introduced	1952
Height	16in/40cm

Some of the brightest greigii are bi-colours. In my opinion the most beautiful is 'Roseanna', which opens red and white and flowers-off pink. Inside the centre is yellow with a red ring and brownish blotches and also flowers of pink. This variety attracts attention year after year. 'Cape Cod' is a reddish apricot edged yellow with a narrow band of apricot along the middle of the petals on the inside. The centre is black with a reddish apricot ring around it. 'Plaisir' is red edged sulphur both inside and out with a black and yellow base. It is a very good grower. 'Pinocchio' is somewhat similar in appearance with a white edge, and is rather cheaper. 'Yellow Dawn' has an urn shape and is carmine rose edged custard yellow. Its base is yellow with a black edge and a rim of blood red. It is a very good grower and very reliable. 'Carioca' has a very similar flower to 'Yellow Dawn' but is somewhat larger and taller. 'Golden Day', one of the best growers in this section, is red edged lemon. Two dwarf cultivars which

PLAISIR	
Classification	Greigii
Year introduced	1953
Height	9in/22.5cm

seem to grow out of the foliage are 'Sun Dance' a vermilion edged saffron and 'Treasure' a tangerine red edged orange. Many of these varieties have good foliage. Two with very exceptional foliage and rather unexceptional blooms are 'Donna Bella' and 'China Lady'.

There are so many reds in this section that only a few can be mentioned. 'Oriental Beauty' is blood red with a deep brown base. It is old, good and one of the smallest. 'Majestic' is a scarlet giant about the size of a Darwin hybrid. Three others that have performed well are 'Cherubina', 'Dr van Hesteren' and 'Red Reflection'.

Of the other taller greigii, 'Corsage' has a wonderfully beautiful bloom but it has a somewhat weak stem. The yellow and red 'Juri Gagarin' is the same. The two tallest have fine rigid stems. These are 'Margaret Herbst' (red) and 'Oriental Splendor' (red and lemon). There seems to be a great deal of breeding continuing in this section. I have seen a number of cultivars that appear to be very good. They are not yet on the market so I have not tested them but there are bound to be some new ones on sale before this book is published. Every year one or two new greigii are available on sale.

Tarda
~

OTHER SPECIES OR TULIPAS

Tulipas are sometimes called wild tulips. To avoid any confusion by conservationists it must be made clear that most of these species were brought into western Europe two, three or even four centuries ago. Many of the reputable bulb growers state in their catalogues that all their species tulips have been grown in their nurseries, in many cases for a very long time. One look at the price of some of these species shows that it would not be practical to send an expedition to central Asia to dig up 10 tulips at the price they are charging.

All these other species must now be considered rather less important than the three in the last chapter – kaufmanniana, fosteriana and greigii. But crossbreeding does takes place and only just over 20 years ago batalinii, eichleri, marjolettii and tubergeniana varieties and hybrids all had their own section in the classified list. These other four are now included in the section 'other species'.

In the latest list there are 205 names. Many of these are for connoisseurs only, being extremely rare and – if available at all – exorbitantly priced. They are usually called small species. Most are, but the tubergeniana varieties and hybrids are giants and several others are of a very significant size.

Over the years biologists have disagreed on the exact affinities and botanical alliances of some of these species. There are also considerable variations in the wild. In some cases the particular colours and types for sale are those that have been selected in nurseries in Holland or perhaps England from the available variations. Even without specific crossbreeding some of the seedlings from some of these species still give extremely variable results. Undoubtedly some degree of crossbreeding does take place. It is also believed that in Persia, where many of these species originate, there was crossbreeding at some time in the past, though little documentation is available.

Usually the first tulip to bloom is *Tulipa pulchella humilis,* until relatively recently simply called *T. humilis.* The common form usually on sale now is a deep violet pink with a yellow centre, though only 60 years ago it was described as a pale rose or lilac. *T. pulchella* 'Eastern Star' is magenta rose with a bronze green flame outside and *T. pulchella* 'Odalisque' is pale purple. *T. pulchella* 'Persian Pearl' is magenta rose with a greenish tinge and *T. pulchella violacea* is cyclamen violet purple. All these cultivars have a yellow base, but *T. pulchella violacea* is also known with a black base. Otherwise it is similar to the other cultivars. These two varieties are listed separately in the classified list.

These pulchella cultivars are popularly called crocus tulips. The cynics among us have observed that crocuses are cheaper.

Next to bloom are two white multiflowering cultivars, *T. biflora* and *T. turkestanica*. They both have small white flowers with a hint of green. Biflora has up to five blooms per stem and turkestanica up to nine. Two very dwarf multiflowered species which are rather similar in habit are *T, urumiensis* (clear yellow) and *T. tarda* (mostly white). Other multiflowering species are *T. hageri* 'Splendens' (dark bronze) and *T. orphanidea* var. *flava* (light bronze), which are from related families. The former may have up to five blooms per stem the latter usually fewer. *T. polychroma* is similar to *T. biflora* but rather larger, much later to bloom and much more expensive. The brightest of all the small multi-flowered species are the *T. praestans* varieties and hybrids. They are all good growers and have up to six blooms per stem. 'Ispahan' is orange, 'Zwanenburg' is vermilion and the tallest of the bunch; while the rest are orange scarlet. 'Fusilier' has well-shaped flowers and its sport 'Unicum' has variegated leaves with a sulphur edge, but among these, probably the best value for money is 'Van Tubergen's Variety'

PULCHELLA HUMILIS	
Classification	Other species
Year introduced	1982
Height	4in/10cm

PULCHELLA VIOLACEA	
Classification	Other species
Height	4in/10cm

TULIPA BIFLORA
Notice how small it is next to the hybrid tulip.
~

BIFLORA	
Classification	Other species
Height	7in/17.5cm

URUMIENSIS	
Classification	Other species
Year introduced	c1932
Height	5in/12.5cm
Awards	FCC W 70

TARDA	
Classification	Other species
Height	4in/10cm
Awards	AM H 37 AM W 70

PRAESTANS 'FUSILIER'	
Classification	Species
Height	10in/25cm
Awards	FCC H 42 AM W 66

Still multiflowered but very much larger in habit, as far as bloom and height are concerned, are the tubergeniana hybrids. Six were introduced between 1951 and 1955 by Jan Roes. 'Oriental Queen' received a First Class Certificate in Haarlem and 'Moustapha' and 'Emir' received the Award of Merit. At the same time tubergeniana hybrids were given their own division in the classified list but this has now ceased and most of the hybrids are difficult to obtain. 'Emir' is oriental red, 'Candidate' is vermilion and 'Keukenhof' is scarlet. They are all very large and beautiful with up to five flowers per stem. It is a great pity that they are not more freely available.

T. clusiana has been in cultivation in the West since 1606 and apparently came from Persia. It has acquired two popular names, the candlestick tulip and the lady tulip. It grows wild in many areas, which is strange as it does not set seed. It is, however, considerably variable in the wild.

The cultivar 'Cynthia' has a chartreuse green edge to the red. In the same group, *T. clusiana* var. *chrysantha* is crimson outside and deep yellow inside. *T. kolpakowskiana* is carmine edged yellow. *T. whittallii* is bronze orange and buff and *T. hageri* is red with a greenish centre. *T. celsiana* is very dwarf, red and yellow with prostate leaves and *T. schrenkii* is red with an orange margin. A good deal larger than these is *T. eichleri,* scarlet, which is stated to be related to the fosteriana. Larger still is *T. eichleri* 'Excelsa'. *T. marjolettii* is yellow with red edges and is much taller. *T. vvedenskyi* comes from Russia, is very large and is in shades of orange and red. The new cultivar vvedenskyi 'Tangerine Beauty', introduced only in 1980, is large and blooms as late as June. Its spectacular flowers have inner petals of bright orange and buff yellow shaded orange outer petals.

CLUSIANA VAR. CHRYSANTHA	
Classification	Species
Height	8in/20cm
Awards	AM H 32 AM W 70

KOLPAKOWSKIANA	
Classification	Species
Height	6in/15cm

EICHLERI 'CLARA BENEDICT'	
Classification	Species
Year introduced	1956
Height	10in/25cm

LINIFOLIA	
Classification	Other species
Height	5in/12.5cm
Awards	AM H 32 AM W 70

There are three small lilac species. *T. saxatilis* (rose lilac) is unfortunately rather shy to flower. *T. aucheriana* is lilac pink and possibly the best is *T. bakeri* Lilac Wonder. There are also five small red May-flowering species: *T. maximowiczii, T. didieri, T. mauritiana, T. ostrowskiana* and *T. wilsoniana*. Finally come the splendid *T. linifolia* (scarlet) and *T. batalinii* (lemon). The classified list states that batalinii is probably the yellow form of *T. linifolia*. Certainly the two hybridize very easily although no hybrids have been found in the wild.

In the early part of the century W. R. Dykes raised a large number of hybrids. They ranged in colour from almost completely yellow to almost completely red, but they were neither named nor described. In 1952, two hybrids were introduced, 'Bronze Charm' from van Tubergen and 'Bright Gem' from Jan Roes. Shortly afterwards two sports were derived from 'Bright Gem' – 'Apricot Jewel' and 'Yellow Jewel'. About this time *T. batalinii* was given its own classified list section. These four hybrids are much more robust than the original species, and will grow almost anywhere. The original species will naturalize satisfactorily only with the special drainage mentioned in the chapter on cultivation.

1985 saw the introduction of a new cultivar, *T. batalinii* 'Red Gem' (often called 'Red Jewel'). This seems slightly less robust than the previous four, and special drainage should be provided if it is to be naturalized.

Most of the tulipas require either special drainage or to be grown in raised beds or rockeries. Those that will naturalize anywhere in addition to the four batalinii hybrids mentioned above are *T. biflora, T. turkestanica* and all the *T. praestans* varieties and hybrids.

BAKERI 'LILAC WONDER'	
Classification	Other species
Year introduced	1971
Height	6in/15cm
Awards	FCC H 77

BATALINII	
Classification	Other species
Height	5in/12.5cm
Awards	AM H 00 FCC W 70

Acuminata

~

SPECIAL EFFECTS
FLOWER SHAPE AND FOLIAGE COLOUR

When Ogier de Busbecq first saw tulips in 1554 he wrote that 'tulips had little or no smell but are admired for the beauty and variety of their colours'. The Turks paid great attention to the shape of their blooms and this has been followed throughout history.

Although a few strong tulips will show eight petals in two sets, most have six petals in two sets. The outer three are generally broader at the base and show a rounder outline as they spring from the stem while the inner three are narrower at the base and more wedge-shaped. The petals of most of the species are long and pointed, but this shape has been modified in many of the garden tulips.

The Turks preferred the lyre or almond shape, and each petal had to resemble a pointed dagger. The three outside petals had to be broader than the inner three but they all had to be of the same length and they all had to touch each other.

The earliest known illustration of a tulip appeared in Conrad Gesner's *'De Hortis . . .'* (1561). It really looks more like a renunculus than a tulip although the leaves resemble the leaves of some tulip species. As the garden tulips were developed all kinds of shapes appeared. The Dutch florists tulips were originally somewhat pointed in petal shape but gradually they became more oval or egg-shaped, like quite a number of the single late tulips. The English florists tulip however was much rounder, the ideal shape being defined as the half of a hollow ball, but a true hemisphere is somewhat shallower in the cup than is usual or desirable, and the typical shape lies somewhere between the hemisphere and the shape of a claret glass.

A double tulip is mentioned as early as 1665, although there is little more reference for a couple of centuries. It is known that in the early days the double tulips had necks which would not support the weight of the flower and were therefore not highly prized. The number of petals required to qualify as a double tulip seems to be nowhere defined. From 1620 there are descriptions of tulips that may possibly be parrot tulips, but they certainly appeared in 1665 and there are two varieties still in cultivation from that date. They were well recognized by the end of that century. Parrot tulips have laciniate flowers and like the doubles, the early ones had weak necks and could not support the bloom.

The lily-flowering tulips with waisted flowers and pointed reflex petals are centuries old. The retroflexa was first introduced by Vincent van der Vinne (1799–1879) of Haarlem. The flower was described as having a fleur-de-lis shape. Many crossings with Darwins and some with cottage tulips have been carried out, and there are now many attractive varieties which are very popular with gardeners and flower arrangers.

The Darwin tulips introduced at the end of the last century started a new trend. Essentially they were cup-shaped but with much squarer shoulders: there is a square bend of the petals where they join the stem.

More recently still, the fringed tulips have become very popular. The early ones were all sports but now the lacy edges to the petals have become very popular and considerable breeding has been done. Another fashion change has been the return of the popularity of the open star shape or flat star shape originally seen in the wild tulips and now a feature of the botanical hybrids, notably the kaufmanniana hybrids which are called water lily tulips.

There are, however, a number of apparently unique shapes which are well worth mentioning. First of all there is *Tulipa acuminata,* a cottage tulip described as a pseudospecies because it has never been seen in the wild. It is also called the horned tulip. This tulip is curious: the long, very narrow tapering petals end in an almost thread-like point. The long flower is yellow streaked with orange-red and grows to about 12 in (30 cm) in May. The single late tulip 'Picture' is unique and long-lasting, having the thickest petals of all tulips. The bright cerise red petals are laciniated and roll slightly inwards, giving a fascinating and distinct shape. Although quite distinct from the parrot tulips, it developed in the same way, being a sport of 'Princess Elizabeth'.

ACUMINATA	
Classification	Species
Height	18in/45cm

There have recently been two sports of 'Apeldoorn' giving a different shape. 'Exotic Bird' (1986) is described as cyclamen shaped and it is red. 'Apeldoorn's Favourite' is semi-double and it is scarlet flushed purple. Another very useful semi-double of course is 'Duplosa', a kaufmanniana hybrid.

MULTIFLORA

These multiflowered tulips are also called branched or branching or even bunching tulips. In the RHS report on nomenclature in 1917 there was a note on these tulips in which they gave an example of 'Monsieur S. Mottet', which is creamy white and undated in the classified list. There is another undated specimen in the classified list – 'Wallflower' (purple brown). It was introduced by Nicholas Dames and his other introductions, 'Rose Mist' (white mottled rose) and 'Madame Mottet' (tyrian purple) were both introduced in 1942.

GEORGETTE	
Classification	Single late
Year introduced	1952
Height	20in/50cm

In 1952 C. V. Hybrida introduced 'Claudette' (white edged red) and 'Georgette' (yellow edged red). 'Georgette' is one of the most successful in this section and has produced two good sports, 'Trenette' (cardinal red) and 'Red Georgette' (very fine clear red).

ORANGE BOUQUET	
Classification	Single late
Year introduced	1964
Height	20in/50cm

'Royal Command' (lake red) and 'Golden Fleece' (buttercup) arrived in 1958. In 1964 'Orange Bouquet' (geranium lake) and 'Fiery Bouquet' (raspberry red and tomato red) were introduced.

Two more were introduced in 1975. 'Modern Style' is ivory white with cyclamen purple blotches and flames. 'Delphi' is ivory white with cobalt violet flame ribbed ruby red. This flower fades into imperial purple with fuchsian spots on a white ground.

All the above were classified cottage tulips and are now single lates, but we now have 'Happy Family' in rosene pink blooming about a fortnight earlier and classified as a Triumph. In some catalogues some botanical tulips may be included in this section. They include greigii tulips 'Toronto' and 'Silvia Warder', together with any tubergiana hybrids they may have to offer.

FOLIAGE COLOUR

The great majority of tulips have green foliage but this may be more or less grey green or bluish green. In the case of kaufmaniana 'Franz Lehar', the leaves are distinctly bluish with purple stripes.

A number of species tulips have bright glossy green leaves, saxatilis being an obvious example. Probably the most attractive in this series is fosteriana 'Cantata', one of the clones selected from the wild. Another in the same category is 'Flaming Youth' also selected from the wild. It is probably less attractive and certainly much less popular than Cantata.

Many of the most attractive leaves are the result of hybridizing *T. greigii*. The species itself has attractive purplish brown spots or marks, but the most beautiful leaves can be found in some of the hybrids between greigii and kaufmaniana or greigii and fosteriana.

T. micheliana and *T. regelii* also have marked leaves but I am no aware that these have been used for serious hybridizing work. O the kaufmaniana tulips, 'Franz Lehar' has already been mentioned and 'Heart's Delight' is another attractive leaved plant Possibly the most beautiful leaves are the fosteriana × greigi hybrids raised by van Tubergen in 1961. Outstanding are 'Juan and 'Toulon'. It is strange that 'Grand Prix', although from the same raiser and giving the same cross of fosteriana × greigii shows virtually no sign of marking on the green leaves. It also blooms much earlier than the others. In the greigii hybrids themselves my personal preference for foliage is 'Oratorio', which also has a good bloom, but other good ones are 'Donna Bella and 'China Lady'.

FRANZ LEHAR	
Classification	Kaufmanniana
Year introduced	1955
Height	7in/17.5cm

NEW DESIGN	
Classification	Triumph
Year introduced	1974
Height	18in/45cm

In recent years three sports have shown a complete change by producing a leaf with a different coloured edge. 'Esperanto' (1968) is a sport of 'Hollywood'. The leaves are edged silvery white. 'New Design' (1974) is a sport of 'Dutch Princess'. The edges of the leaf opens quite pink when the leaves first show through, later fading to pinkish white. 'Praestans Unicom' (1975) is a sport of 'Fusilier'. The edge of the leaves is sulphur yellow. All three of these new sports are attractive flowers as well as attractive foliage and they should all now be quite reasonable in price.

PRAESTANS 'UNICUM'	
Classification	Other species
Year introduced	1975
Height	12in/30cm

Dawnglow
~

THE REPRODUCTION OF TULIPS

The tulip is reproduced in three ways. Vegetative reproduction is the norm, but most varieties and cultivars can be reproduced from seed, though there are some which are infertile. Thirdly there is the vegetative mutation or sport, which creates a new cultivar from the old. There was a time when the breaking of tulips was regarded as a mutation or sport, but it is now accepted as being a form of disease.

Once a variety or cultivar is established more tulips of exactly the same type are produced by vegetative reproduction. New varieties can be produced only by raising seedlings which will be dealt with at the end of this chapter, or by sports. The majority of sports involve only a colour change, as in the case of the more than 100 sports of 'Murillo'. But a sport may involve a complete change in shape as, for example, when a single flower gives a sport which is fully double. Others such as 'Apeldoorn' have given sports which are semi-double. 'Apeldoorn' has also sported to give 'Exotic Bird' which is described as a cyclamen shaped flower. The unusually shaped 'Picture' is a sport of 'Queen Elizabeth'; many of the fringed tulips are sports; and all parrot tulips are sports. The single late tulip 'Golden Harvest' has produced two parrot sports, 'Sensation' and 'Yellow Parrot'. It has also produced an excellent fully double late tulip called 'Ostara', which is lemon yellow like its parent.

The exact cause of sports is unknown, though considerable experimentation has been carried out. According to one report the parrot tulip 'Estella Rijnveld' (syn. 'Gay Presto') was developed from 'Red Champion' by a Dr De Mol through radiation treatments. I am not aware if any further experiments along these lines have taken place.

Purissima, with its sport Sweetheart and Candela.

~

*A selection of sports; Daydream, Oxford's Elite,
Oxford and Jewel of Spring.*

~

MORPHOLOGY

This is a botanical term meaning the science of the form of the
plant together with the structures, correspondences and changes
governing or influencing that form. The fully developed tulip
plant is composed of a bulb with roots and a flowering shoot,
consisting of a stem, leaves and one or more flowers.

The bulb is a specialized organ for vegetative reproduction,
serving at the same time as the plant's food store. The disc-shaped
stem of the bulb is called the basal plate. The reserve material is
stored in specialized fleshy leaf bases or 'fleshy scales', varying in
number from one in juvenile to six in adult plants. On the outside the bulb is covered by another specialized scale, the tunic.
Dead scales of previous years clothe the tulip bulb, protected
from unfavourable external conditions.

Within the fleshy scales lies the apical bud of the adult bulb which develops into the flowering shoot. Below the fleshy scale is an axil with the bud for the main daughter bulb which will replace the mother bud for the following year. Other small bulbs may initiate in the axils of other fleshy scales: these daughter bulbs or 'offset' bulbs are the means of vegetative reproduction.

When a tulip bulb is planted the apical bud, or growing point, gradually pushes upwards until it emerges from the soil, still apparently as a solid point, but when about an inch (2.5 cm) high it splits vertically and begins to show its character of a folded leaf, which gradually expands and flattens. A second leaf soon emerges, folded so as to face the fold of the outer most leaf, and between the two rises a central stalk, terminated eventually by the flower bud. A tulip that is not going to flower in that season will only throw up a single leaf, which is called a cotyledon. The old florists called these non-flowering tulips 'widows'.

As the flower stem elongates it will be found to carry two or three leaves, those springing from higher up the stem being narrower and more pointed. Usually the stem carries only a single flower, but with a few varieties it may branch into two or three stems with flowers of varying size. If two or more stems spring from the same bulb they probably arise from large offsets which have not been separated before planting.

The structure of the flower itself is simple; the perianth is made up of six segments or petals. These, though they form a symmetrical cup, are arranged in two sets of three, outer and inner, differing somewhat in shape. Within the perianth are six stamens, consisting of large anthers set end-wise upon filaments springing from the base of the flower. The filament terminates in a fine point which fits into a cavity in the base of the anther. The filaments encircle a large triangular ovary which as a rule possess no style, but terminates in the stigmatic surface. This surface may be small, a simple folding over of the style, or it may spread into an almost furry series of convolutions, overlapping the ovary.

Often the stamens of the tulip burst open and the pollen of the tulips is ready to shed as soon as the flower opens, but the stigmatic surface is usually not ready for the reception of the pollen for two or three days later.

Lifted bulbs, showing both main and subsidiary bulbs.
~

The stages of development, from seed to maturity, takes place over a period of six years.
~

Labelled capsules.
~

Many tulips are self-fertile: the pollen and egg cell of the same flower or between different individuals of the same clone may produce the seed. Or there may be a normal crossing between seedling individuals of the same species. If the union is between different varieties of the same species or race, the progeny should be called crossbreeds, and finally crossing between two different species gives rise to hybrids. These words may be used quite loosely however. We still have quite a number of points to learn about hybridism between different kinds of *Tulipa* species, but the many varieties that we call the garden tulip are usually quite fertile between themselves.

When fertilized the tulip produces its fruit, which is a capsule formed by the superior ovary in which two horizontal layers of flat seeds are attached to the end curved edges. As the seeds ripen the capsule easily splits open and the seeds may fall out. Gardeners who do not wish seeds should prevent them from forming.

When the flowering has finished and the foliage begins to wither and the plants are lifted, removing the tunic will reveal that the old mother bulb has been replaced by a new daughter bulb, sometimes by two or three, but normally by one main daughter bulb and a number of subsidiary daughter bulbs. The main daughter bulbs will provide the opportunity for next year's flowers and the smaller daughter bulbs or offsets can be grown for a year or two as is indicated in the chapter on cultivation. These offsets originate from the dormant buds on the old bulb.

SEEDLINGS AND DROPPERS

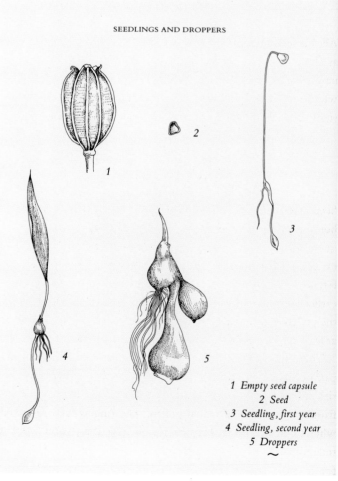

1 Empty seed capsule
2 Seed
3 Seedling, first year
4 Seedling, second year
5 Droppers
~

HIGHLY RECOMMENDED TULIPS ABOVE STANDARD PRICES

CLASSIFICATION GROUP	NAME	DATE	COLOUR	AWARDS	HEIGHT
1	Silver Standard	1637	white/rose-red		11in/27.5
4	Canopus	1945	red		23in/57.5cm
4	Tender Beauty	c.1951	white/rosy red	AM W 54	20in/50cm
5	Picture	1949	lilac-rose		20in/50cm
6	Picotee	1895	white/pink		19in/47.5cm
7	Johann Gutenberg	1970	indian-lake/white		26in/65cm
8	viridiflora praecox	post 1700	yellow/green		18in/45cm
12	Fritz Kreisler	1942	pink/mauve/sulphur	AM H 42. FCC W 66	14in/35cm
12	Goudstuk	1952	carmine/gold	AM W 66	12in/30cm
12	Duplosa	1955	raspberry-red		9in/22.5cm
13	Reginald Dixon	1955	scarlet/yellow		15in/37.5cm
14	Sweet Lady	1955	peach blossom		9in/22.5cm
15	aucheriana		mauve-lilac	AM W 70	12in/30cm
15	polychroma		white/violet		6in/15cm
15	celsiana		yellow/bronze	AM W 70	5in/12.5cm

All the new bulbs and offsets – large and small – can be described as clones because they are produced asexually and are therefore new parts of an old plant. In this way many millions of tulips which are virtually identical to one another can be grown from a single bulb. This is the vegetative propagation system.

BREEDING AND SEEDLING RAISING

Seedlings are more successful if the gardener has a cool greenhouse available. Although attacks from botrytis are not so frequent as they once were, the cool greenhouse makes it much easier to bring together tulips which bloom at considerably different times if they are grown in pots. It is often easier to use earlier blooming plants as the seed bearers and anything later as the pollen bearers because normally the pollen becomes available at least three or four days before the stigmatic surface is ready.

The anthers of the female parent are carefully picked out with a pair of forceps and thrown away. The stigmatic surface and ovaries are then enclosed in a ball of loose cotton wool to protect it from the invasion of casual pollen. The ring is then removed, whereupon the petals may be closed over the cotton wool to retain it and secure it. The emasculated flowers will not be ready for fertilization for a week or more. The anthers of the male

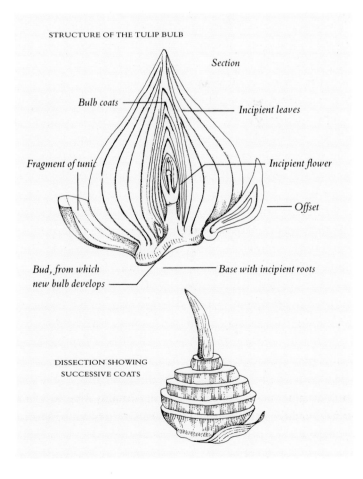

STRUCTURE OF THE TULIP BULB

Section

Bulb coats — *Incipient leaves*

Fragment of tunic — *Incipient flower*

— *Offset*

Bud, from which new bulb develops — *Base with incipient roots*

DISSECTION SHOWING SUCCESSIVE COATS

parent must be removed before the pollen is released and also before any foreign pollen could be brought in by bees or other insects. The anthers will be removed in the same way as the anthers of the female parent but in this case they are carefully stored, perhaps in a small plastic box, until the stigmatic surface of the female parent is ready for the reception of pollen. When it is ready it begins to look sticky and shiny. The pollen from the male parent is then transferred, preferably by means of a camel-haired brush, and transferred to the stigma of the female parent until it is thoroughly covered. If the sigma is ready the pollen will stick to it quite happily. If the adhesion is not perfect the process should be repeated a day or two later. The ball of cotton wool may then be replaced. The flower should be examined on the following day. If fertilization has taken place there will be a change of colour and the stigmatic surface will have dried.

Now one can await the development of the seed. The pots should be judiciously watered, but gradually dried off and the atmosphere should be kept dry. The seed pod will rapidly swell and must be left to ripen; the process is generally complete when the seeds can be seen through the outside of the pod, which then begins to split from the top.

When to sow the seed has been a matter of some dispute. The old English florists waited until the following spring, but Sir Daniel Hall believes that autumn is definitely preferable and that it is probably better still to sow the seed immediately it is ripe. Seed pans should be filled with 3 in (75 mm) of open friable soil, the seed should be soaked in water for 24 hours and sown about ¼ in (6mm) deep. The seed pans should be covered with a pane of glass to conserve moisture and may be placed on the shady side of a hedge or wall or in a cold frame. The essential thing is to prevent the soil from ever drying out. Protection should not be given since germination often improves after the pans have been exposed to frost. Germination should normally begin in the late autumn or in the early months of the new year; the thin rush-like leaves, each carrying the empty seed coat on its tip, should come up thickly. When germination has begun the seed pans may be removed to a cold frame but the ventilation should be carefully attended to or damping off may destroy many of the seedlings. For the same reason watering should continue from below.

As the leaves begin to flag there should be a few weeks of complete dryness and sun baking of the pans. Towards the end of May the small one-year-old bulbs can be gathered up, stored in sand and planted in early autumn, 3in (75mm) deep in a box which is filled with about 5 in (12.5 cm) of light soil. The one essential again is that boxes should not be allowed to dry out but they should also not be allowed to become too wet. Protection

SAXATILIS	
Classification	Species
Height	6in/15cm
Awards	AM W 1896

MRS JOHN T SCHEEPERS	
Classification	Single late
Year introduced	1930
Height	24in/60cm
Awards	FCC H 31

gainst botrytis is essential. For the second time the pans are urned out and the bulbs bagged up, afterwards for the third ime they are again put into boxes for the next year's growth.

The fourth year's growth should be in the open ground on a vell-worked piece of land, which should be hoed continuously eady for planting in early autumn. Under normal conditions a ew plants will flower in the fifth year and the majority of the rest n the sixth year when the whole batch should be dug up and the irst selection made. Selection should not be too ruthless in the irst year because they have not had a fair chance to produce their est in that time; only those that are obviously useless should be hrown away. After each successive year's growth some varieties nay be rogued away but you will need at least two or three years o see if a new variety has a really good constitution.

POLYPLOIDY

In recent years much work has been done by botanists to determine the chromosome numbers of several hundred of tulip species and cultivars. Many chromosome numbers are now included in the classified list.

The basic haploid chromosome number for tulips is 12, the great majority of tulips are diploids ($2n = 24$). Among tulipas there are some cases of increases and reductions in the basic numbers of chromosomes. A reduction was found in *Tulipa maximowiczii* where the number of chromosomes is 11, so that $2n = 22$. *Tulipa lanata* varies considerably, in some cases $2n = 22$, in some cases $2n = 24$ and in others $2n = 36$.

The greater part of the cultivars of garden tulips appear to be diploid but the number of triploid (36 chromosomes) is increasing year by year. The robust and vigorous Darwin hybrids, with only two exceptions, are all triploids. There are also a number of single late and Triumph tulips. During the last few years many crosses were made within these groups, but not many tetraploid cultivars have been determined.

The Royal General Dutch Bulb Growers' Association (KAVB) has published many tulip parentages. These show that frequently diploids crossed with diploids repeatedly produce triploid seedlings. Many triploids now appear in the classified list, but not all are recent. For example, the old cottage variety 'Inglescombe Yellow' and its sports are in there. There are only six tulipa species in the triploid list, whereas among the tetraploids there are nine, and only a relatively small number of cultivated tulips.

It has long been thought that polyploidy tended to create strong and robust tulips, but this has not been proved with any certainty. Nevertheless, for those who wish to sow their seeds and choose the parents of their seedlings, this list is very valuable.

TURKESTANICA	
Classification	Other species
Height	9in/22.5cm

SYLVESTRIS	
Classification	Species
Height	11in/27.5cm

Bulbfields near Lisse in Holland.

CULTIVATION

Tulips respond well to ordinary good husbandry and this chapter will attempt to cover the problems and answers.

First there must be a decision on the chief function the tulips are to serve. They can be for garden display, for cut flowers or for indoors, or perhaps a combination of all three. For a combination it is best to have the garden display in the main beds or those near the house, with cut flowers in the vegetable plot. This book is primarily concerned with garden decoration, but will try to deal with all three and even with a fourth function, bulb production.

The next decision is what sort of flowers to acquire, small or large, early or late, short or tall and finally which colours and shapes. The main suppliers issue catalogues from spring to early autumn. Bulbs should arrive during early autumn when bulbs also appear in the local garden centres, corner shops and larger stores. Some advice on suitable cultivars is given in the chapters on each class of tulips and two sets of recommendations are given in the previous chapter.

Bulbs are sold by size, as measured by their circumference in centimetres. A size 10 bulb has a circumference of 4 in (about 10 cm). Sizes 11 and 12 are recommended for good results; size 12 is good for indoor work. Botanical and wild tulips are an exception to this rule. They may be no larger than size 3 or 4.

Bulbs are normally available with a brown outer skin. With some cultivars this skin tears easily. This does not matter in itself but may allow fungus or disease to enter. Such bulbs should be examined. Bulbs with torn skins are called untidy. They bruise easily and the Dutch say they should be handled like eggs.

Tulips may be grown in a bed of their own or with spring flowering plants such as wallflowers, forget-me-nots, arabis, lobelias or pansies. They may also be introduced into a herbaceous border. Many gardeners prefer curves, and clumps of tulips may be grown in circles, ovals or crescents. It is a matter of personal taste, but usually rectangles of bulbs will allow the maximum to be planted.

Tulips are normally planted and lifted each year. Most tulips prefer this. Tulips are more mobile than daffodils and are happy to be out of the ground longer.

The only flowers I grow in any quantity with my tulips are daffodils. They go very well together and are completely compatible. Tulips should not be planted until the middle of autumn by which time the daffodils should all be in.

Finally, before starting the work of planting, remember that you will need probably double the amount of time to lift the bulbs again between April and June.

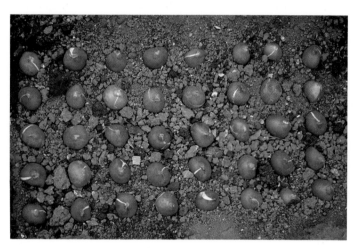

Planting starts.

PLANTING

In the northern Hemisphere, north of 30° latitude, the ideal planting months are October and November. Earlier planting increases the risk of disease. In Australia and New Zealand there is a time difference of approximately six months. Their autumn starts in March and spring in September. In hotter areas, there is more flexibility, but it is desirable that all bulbs should be stored at a temperature of about 40°F for about eight weeks before planting. This would include the southern states of the USA and northern Australia.

The ground must first be thoroughly dug, preferably to a depth of 18 in (45 cm). Tulips need good drainage, but there is a distinction between normal good drainage and special drainage for certain cultivars. Most modern hybrids will fare very well in any normal garden, but if there is any danger of the bulbs becoming waterlogged then some grit or stones should be added at a depth of 18in (45cm) before the soil is returned. Special drainage is more thorough. I have a number of slabs of thin concrete from an old broken path. Round several of my beds I have created an edging 10–12 in wide (25–30 cm). Here I have placed these broken slabs about 14 in (35 cm) down and then replaced the soil. Broken bricks, tiles or slates would do equally well, and provide an excellent situation for those cultivars or wild tulips which need this special drainage.

All plants need nutrients. Tulips are not gross feeders, and the administration of nutrients should be carried out with restraint. Fresh manure, whether stable or farmyard, should never be used. Even thoroughly rotted manure should be used very sparingly. Some humus in the ground is helpful and for several years peat has been a firm favourite. Today some environmentalists are pointing out that excessive extraction of peat causes irreversible problems. Substitutes for peat are shredded bark or perlite, rotted leaf mould, garden compost or fibrous loam. Wood ash is also helpful. If fertilizers are used, superphosphates or sulphate of potash are best. There should be a maximum of 5 per cent nitrogen in compound fertilizers. Bonemeal or hoof and horn are very good to use.

Special drainage system.

Most planting is done with a spade for a clump of bulbs or a trowel for single items. A dibber is sometimes used and there are also special hand- or foot-operated tools for planting individual bulbs. They extract a tube of soil. The bulb is planted and the tube of soil replaced. There is sometimes a handle to expel the tube of soil if it sticks. Although these tools were probably designed for planting daffodils in grass, tulips should not be grown in grass. A few will survive but not thrive. On clay or heavy soil tulips should be planted 3–4 in (8–10 cm) deep and on lighter soils an inch or two more.

I prefer to remove the topsoil completely with a spade to the required depth, plant the bulbs, which I cover lightly with soil, and sprinkle with bonemeal before returning the rest of the soil.

It is important to leave space to walk among the growing stems and flowers. They must be closely observed to see if any spraying is needed. It is also necessary when the blooms open to mark any rogues or Rembrandts with coloured string, wool or tie twists. You may also find it desirable to mark the whereabouts of what you have planted with labels. Better still is a rough sketch plan on which all relevant plantings can be shown. If bulbs are to be naturalized – not lifted each year – they should be planted deeper, perhaps as much as 9 or 10 in (28 or 30 cm).

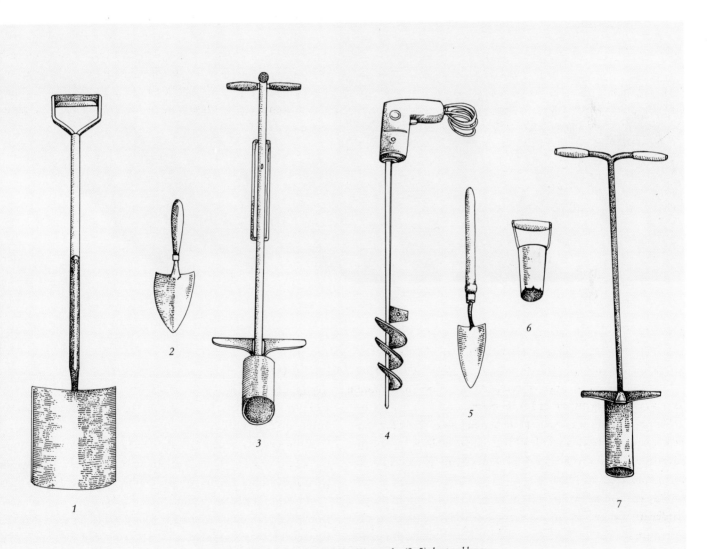

Planting tools on the market include, (1) a spade, (2, 5) short and long handled trowels, (3, 6, 7) large and small bulb planters, and (4) a drill attachment for planting deep bulbs.

~

Cut tulips from a florist.

Blooms for indoors

Tulips for cutting, whether for the house or for show, are best grown in rows in some part of the garden away from the show beds, or in the kitchen garden. The old tradition is to have the rows about 3½–4 ft (85 cm–1 m) wide. Many gardeners define them with creosoted boards 8 in (20 cm) deep and kept in position by crossboards at intervals of about 15 ft (4.5 m). In the past gardeners changed the topsoil every year where tulips are grown to reduce the risk of Tulip Fire, and the boards made this easier. However, the prevalent use now of systemic fungicide lets the same topsoil be used year after year.

Where boards are used it is easy to plant the bulbs at ground level and then cover them with 4–5 in (10–12.5 cm) of soil kept in place by the boards. Otherwise just dig a trench with the spade and plant as normal. It is better that rows run north–south with ample space to walk between them.

Some kind of screen may be erected before flowering time if the site is windy. Remember, though, to observe competition rules if the tulips are for competition on the show bench.

In warm, dry weather some watering may be required. Occasionally the amount required is considerable. In special circumstances the keen enthusiast may wish to install some permanent irrigation system. If the blooms are covered with glass or polythene, this should not be done before the buds show colour. Again, remember any competition rules to the contrary. Such covering will make the plants seem drawn up and may increase dryness of the beds.

Bulbs for growth indoors

ifty years ago millions of tulips were forced, not only for cut lowers, but also in pots for taking into the house. The number f cut flowers has probably increased, but forcing for pots appears o be rather less popular. This may be partly due to the difficulty f cultivation, or to the very restricted numbers of cultivars vailable for forcing. Forcing is also expensive, since bulbs once orced are virtually useless. Moreover, gardeners can now grow ery early botanical tulips which can be brought indoors without orcing from February onwards. I am told that in some places ots of forced tulips are on sale so that all that remains to be done to take them indoors and enjoy them. No one near me has ever nade such an offer.

The list of tulips that are suitable for forcing on the following page is not exhaustive but it does cover those most freely available. Most tulips cannot be forced at all. Of those that can, some can stand more heat than others. I have divided them into five groups, only the first group being suitable for December forcing. The letters EFA are shown against those cultivars that have received the Early Forcing Award, Haarlem.

First the bulbs must be potted into pots with drainage and good potting soil. Most experts recommend 5-in or 6-in (12–15 cm) pots which can hold three to five and six to eight bulbs respectively. They then rather irritatingly show an illustration of 10 large tulips in a pot which is at least 9–10 in (23–25 cm). I suggest that you try different sizes of pots remembering that the bulbs should be size 12 and should not touch one another. Planting should be earlier than outdoors, perhaps September or even August. The bulbs should be planted firmly with the nose just showing above the soil. Water the pot thoroughly.

Fill a shallow pot halfway with soil.

~

Cover them with soil so that just their tips are visible.

~

Place the tulip bulbs in the pot with the flat side of the tulip pointing towards the side and their pointed end faced upwards.

~

The ideal procedure now is to put the pot in a refrigerator at about 40°F for 10–16 weeks, then place it in a warm place and wait for the blooms. Most people just do not have room in their refrigerators for pots of tulips, so the alternative is three months in a plunge bed. In a cool and well shaded part of the garden, the soil is removed to a depth of about 6 in (15 cm) or more. Pots are placed in this pit and completely covered with 3–4 in (7.5–10 cm) of ashes, fibre or sand. If these are not available, soil will do. The position and contents of each pot must be carefully marked as they must be lifted from the plunge bed about three weeks before being forced and placed in very gentle warmth. Greater heat may be given as they grow. This is easier for those with a greenhouse or even a light garden shed, but it can now be done indoors if excessive heat is avoided. Tulips can be grown in fibre in bowls without drainage but they must still be started outside and protected from rain or the bowls will become waterlogged.

Water them well and store them in a cool, dark place. When they have sprouted between 1–2 in (2.5–5 cm) they should be removed from the cold area.

~

TULIPS SUITABLE FOR FORCING

FOR FORCING LATE DECEMBER	FOR FORCING MID FEBRUARY
'Brilliant Star' with sports 'Joffre' (EFA) and 'Brilliant Star Maxima' 'Christmas Marvel' (EFA) with sports 'Christmas Carol', 'Christmas Dream' and 'Merry Christmas' 'Christmas Gold' (EFA)	'Cassini' 'Kees Nelis' 'Valentine' 'Stockholm' (EFA) 'Monte Carlo' 'Murillo' with sports 'Peach Blossom', 'Orange Nassau', 'Garanza', 'Rheingold' and 97 other sports
FOR FORCING MID JANUARY 'Scarlet Cardinal' 'Diana' 'Early Light' (EFA) 'Sulphur Cloud' (EFA) 'Van der Neer' 'Orange Wonder' with sport 'High Society'	**FOR FORCING LATE FEBRUARY** 'Princess Irene' 'Golden Show' (scented) 'William Copland' with sports 'Rose Copland', 'Copland's Purple' and 8 other sports
FOR FORCING LATE JANUARY 'Apricot Beauty' (EFA) with sports 'Bestseller, 'Jenny' and 'Beauty Queen' 'Blizzard' 'Bellona' 'Doctor Plesman' 'Couleur Cardinal' 'Prince of Austria' with sports 'Prins Carnival' and 'General de Wet' 'Paul Richter' 'Bing Crosby' 'Topscore' (EFA)	*EFA = Early Forcing Award, Haarlem* *(Southern hemisphere, please add approximately six months)*

When placed in the light the foliage will turn green.

~

Forced tulips in bloom.

~

I have even grown them on water alone in a plastic container probably designed for hyacinths. I got eight blooms from ten bulbs. I have not repeated the experiment.

My preferred alternative now is to grow botanical tulips in plastic lattice pots. These comfortably take 10 bulbs and are now available from many suppliers. They are planted up in the usual way in October and need a much shallower plunge bed. As soon as the first bud shows a hint of colour the pot is lifted, brought into the house and placed on a large saucer. Each batch of 10 tulips lasts 7–10 days. Before they die the next pot is ready to bring in.

Because they have not been forced, the bulbs should be quite ready for planting in the beds or borders the following year.

Occasionally several get mixed. When this happens the rogues may be marked by tying different coloured string or wool round the stem below the top leaf. Tie-twists, whose normal function is to secure plants to stakes, are an alternative to string.

When checking rogues, it is just possible that you may find an exciting new sport. This happens rarely, but is well worth preserving when it does.

Rembrandts, or tulips where the colour is broken by a virus, are a much greater problem. The virus is spread by aphis, and if not checked spreads very rapidly. Once the blooms start to die, deadheading must begin. If seedpods are allowed to form they will take all the strength from the bulbs, and the stem should be broken or cut just below the neck. These heads, with all foliage, must be burnt and not composted.

Planting in plastic lattice baskets.

~

GROWTH AND ENJOYMENT

Once the planting is completed, ideally by the end of November, there is little to do for a few weeks. Growth starts appearing above ground soon after the middle of January in a mild winter. A thorough hoeing at the very beginning of the year will prevent a lot of weeds and avoid cutting off the growing tips. Once the foliage shows, a constant watch must be kept for aphis or fungus. The appropriate spraying is outlined in Chapter 13. As the different cultivars come into bloom take pictures, make notes and alterations and additions for the following year. It is also necessary to mark any rogues or Rembrandts. Sometimes tulip bulbs on sale can be picked up from one open box and dropped in another.

Dead-heading using a thumbnail to break the stem.

~

LIFTING

The actual date when lifting starts cannot be given, but it is usually possible towards the end of spring. The foliage of some types seems to die off more quickly than others, and the weather also has its effect. The new bulbs are fed by the action of light on the foliage and the headed stem, so it is undesirable to lift too early. If lifting is too late, the dead foliage separates from the bulb and may be blown about by even a slight breeze. The ideal time for lifting varies from year to year and can be judged by experienced observation. It is of course essential that those bulbs which have been specially marked as rogues, sports or Rembrandts should be lifted before the stem becomes separated from the

Dead-headed tulips.

~

Tulips ready for deadheading.

~

bulbs. Every scrap of foliage must be burnt or Tulip Fire may ravage next year's crop.

While lifting the tulips, the gardener will consider the question of putting summer bedding plants where the tulips have been. Early and very early tulips have become more popular partly for this reason, as some of the latest tulips are still in bloom in June, when most summer bedding plants are ready for planting. I find that bedding dahlias are excellent in the summer. They are completely compatible with the tulip so far as the calendar is concerned. They will also use the same storage.

Finally, it should be mentioned that in dry seasons, or if bulbs are planted too shallow, a stolon leaves the old bulb, goes downward and forms a bulb at the bottom. These 'droppers' are no different from other bulbs, but if lifting is done carelessly, they may be left in the ground and form rogues next year.

STORAGE

When first lifted, bulbs should be labelled and dried. During this drying-off period and in permanent storage the bulbs must have a free circulation of air, not be too hot and must be in an area completely free of mice or other predators. If moist bulbs are kept too hot without adequate ventilation, they may be converted into a sort of hard jelly and be completely destroyed. I place each group of fully dry bulbs into paper bags and place the bags in cardboard boxes. I then take them up into my attic, but any airy mice-free place will do. Most bulbs ordered by post arrive in paper bags, as these allow the bulbs to breathe. Plastic should never be used. Obviously the use of paper makes it essential that the bulbs are dry, otherwise the paper will rot and the bulbs get mixed.

Droppers.

~

Bulb production

When a normally vigorous tulip is lifted, there will be one or two new bulbs for next year's flowering, together with a varying number of offsets, called bulblets or bulbils. These offsets vary in size, some being almost large enough to bloom, down to tiny pieces smaller than a pea. These may be planted in a piece of spare ground and will start to give blooms after 18 months.

I grow mine on a vegetable plot. I take out a long trench about 8 in (20 cm) wide and 3 in (7.5 cm) deep, bundle in the offsets, marking carefully one cultivar from another. If lifted after 18 months, there should be a number of bulbs of flowering size; the remainder can go back with the new offsets. The more robust varieties can be left in for two or three years and provide an excellent source of cut flowers.

Orange Emperor and Toronto.

PESTS AND DISEASES

All tulip growers face the common enemy of plant diseases. Because of the disease inspection services carried out in Holland and elsewhere it is likely that the bulbs on sale will be healthy. However, you should still watch for certain diseases.

TULIP FIRE

This is a fungus disease known as *Botrytis tulipae*. There are two explanations why it is called Tulip Fire. One is that it spreads so fast once started that it has reminded people of prairie fires. The other explanation is that the leaves affected sometimes look as though they are burnt. Traditionally Tulip Fire has been the most important problem affecting tulip growers, but the recent invention and production of systemic fungicides have made an immense difference. It used to be stated that tulips should never be grown in the same soil year after year because of the resting bodies of fungus, but I have now grown tulips in the same soil for 44 years without any serious problems because of the use of systemic fungicides.

A tulip with botrytis.

~

Tulip Fire is first seen as the plants come above ground, affected plants having now malformed leaves and shoots. There is a yellowing or shrivelling of the tips of the leaves together with spots along the edges of the leaves. Crippled shoots wither, cease to develop and soon become covered with grey masses of fungus spores under moist conditions. In severe cases large grey or scorched areas are produced. These are also covered with spores, which spread the infection to the flower stalks. Elongated and depressed lesions develop on the stalks. In extreme cases stalks may be so weakened that the flowers topple over. Spots appear on the petals, usually dark spots on light coloured petals, and in wet weather flowers decay rapidly.

A broken stem.

~

Botrytis attacks tulips most often if the season is warm and wet while the plants are developing. It can be controlled to some extent by the removal of affected leaves and petals. But as soon as such symptoms appear, the plants should be sprayed thoroughly with systemic fungicide. If this does not succeed, pull up the plants and discard them. Resting bodies (sclerotia) of the fungus are produced in vast numbers in the diseased tissues and on the bulbs. These are black and the size of a pin-head. They fall into the soil where they remain viable for several years. All infected leaves and crippled plants should be removed and burnt as soon

as the first symptoms are seen. The sclerotia can be seen on the bulbs when they are lifted. Healthy bulbs should be immersed in a solution of fungicide. The soaking of bulbs in a solution of fungicide before planting should normally eliminate any problems for that year, but it must be emphasized that all dead foliage be removed immediately from the site and burned.

GREY BULB ROT

This is another fungus disease, *Sclerotium tuliparum,* but fortunately it is much less common than botrytis. Bulbs are attacked in the soil and generally fail to come through at all. First indications of the presence of the disease therefore are gaps in the bed. Where a shoot is produced by a diseased bulb, it is severely crippled and soon withers and dies without flowering. No fungus spores are produced on diseased tissues.

The fungus attacks the bulb at the nose and produces a dry greyish rot of the scales, which soon causes the decay of most bulbs, with the exception of the basal plate and roots. The scales remain firm. Between these and on the outside of the bulb there forms a felted mass of whitish fungal growth, in which numerous sclerotia are developed. These are at first soft and white, later becoming dark brown and finally black and hard. They are spherical or flattened and about a quarter of an inch in size. These sclerotia contaminate the soil and remain viable for about three or four years.

If you see gaps in your beds which are otherwise not to be explained, search for the missing bulbs. All rotten bulbs or debris should be examined for the sclerotia to confirm the presence of the disease. The soil is inclined to adhere to affected bulbs, especially at the noses.

If only a few plants are affected, remove and burn them together with the soil around them. Fortunately the same systemic fungicide which eliminates Tulip Fire will also eliminate *Sclerotium tuliparum* if the bulbs are thoroughly soaked in the fungicide before planting.

TBV

This is a virus, and known by many people as Rembrandt virus, but also as TBV or tulip breaking virus. It attacks the bulb and the colour becomes broken. Tulip breaking virus turns a self-coloured tulip into one which is splashed, spotted or striped. It is as if the anthocyanin pigment which was formerly diffused over the whole petal has become gathered up into certain restricted areas, leaving the white or yellow ground between o longer modified by the anthocyanin. This change is called 'breaking', the flower is termed 'broken' or 'rectified', while the original form is known as a 'breeder'.

All the individual bulbs of a particular group or variety do not break at once. The change may affect only a single bulb or perhaps two or three in a large batch. Once broken, however, an individual bulb remains broken and all the offsets from it are also broken. The differentiation between the various kinds of marking is dealt with in detail in Chapter 6. But if the marking is sharply defined, it differs entirely from the flushing of a flower which sometimes spreads over the entire bloom as in the case of the Darwin hybrid tulip 'Daydream'. The marking, however, is not constant. It will vary between different individuals of the same variety and in the same individual from year to year. As compared with the original breeder tulip the colouring is usually much more intense. Pink turns to scarlet, dull slatey purple to a purple approaching black. The base of the flower is quite unaffected by breaking.

The breaking is not confined to the flower; both stem and leaves may be affected. Frequently irregular purple markings can

Daydream – natural colour change.

~

be seen on the stem and the leaves may show a mottled appearance, especially if held up to the light. Since the chlorophyll is gathered up into little irregular clots or patches, sometimes into well-defined stripes or streaks, it may be possible to pick out a broken tulip before the bloom actually opens. However, this is not entirely reliable.

Breaking can also occur to the self-yellows and self-whites even though they contain no anthocyanin pigment. Thus of course it cannot be seen from the bloom. The gardener hopes that mottling of the leaves or of the stem may assist in placing them. Otherwise such varieties will be carriers of the virus, which may then be spread to other blooms.

Breaking is far less common among the early tulips than among the latest, probably because the aphis which spread them are less common in March and April than they are in May and June. I have observed breaking on only two varieties of very early botanical tulips – fosteriana 'Orange Emperor' and tuber-

Aphis on dying foliage.
~

geniana 'Keukenhof'. When breaking occurs there is a slight but definite reduction in the sizes of the bloom and in the height of the stem and in the general vigour of the plant. Broken bulbs also increase less freely so that the virus clearly has an effect upon the vigour of the plant. In an eighteenth-century tulip book, D. H. Cause stated 'experience has shown that an affected bulb produces a flower more beautiful than before and shortly afterwards dies as if it had used its last strength to please its owner'. It has been said that the beauty of such flowers is a beauty of death. However, it is observed that seedlings from broken tulips bloom as if they have been derived from healthy plants.

Clearly seventeenth-century horticulturalists knew nothing whatever about virus diseases. However, they were aware that the presence of insects on plants could create the broken form of tulips. They also discovered that the presence of lice in tulip beds caused breaking. Growers of florist tulips who particularly wanted broken tulips actually created an environment in which aphis flourished on the tulips. There are a number of growers of florists tulips even today and there are societies which promote their growth. But for the majority of gardeners and for the majority of professional bulb growers, tulip breaking virus is a menace as it can spread very rapidly from flower to flower by the influence of insects, particularly aphis. Consequently all growers are recommended to use at a very early stage in growth a systemic insecticide. If necessary they should respray every seven to ten days as the effect of systemic insecticide seems to last for a shorter period than the effect of a systemic fungicide.

Orange Emperor and Toronto.
~

Aphis on a tulip.
~

PREDATORS

In the ground slugs will attack almost all tulips, though in my experience they seem to be particularly fond of certain types. The greigii tulips are notable in this respect, as slugs will not only go for the bulb, but even for the foliage. It does seem that they will also attack the double early tulips more than some of the later ones. If slugs are prevalent in your garden use slug bait or slug pellets, particularly around the most susceptible bulbs.

Mice and other rodents will attack tulips in store, if they are not protected. Many years ago I stored a number of tulips in the garden shed for several years. Suddenly one year the neighbour's cat died without my being aware of it and I lost several valuable stocks of tulips. The one outstanding exception to this was 'Inglescombe Yellow', which the mice did not touch. I have never been able to establish if this was pure coincidence or not. Presumably other rodents would also cause damage. Although heat is not strictly a pest, I have already mentioned the destructive action on a bulb caused by excessive heat without a free flow of air. This can convert the whole interior of a bulb into a mass of hard jelly-like substance.

SUPPLIERS IN GREAT BRITAIN

FRANS ROOZEN B.V., Vogelenzangseweg 49, 2114BB
Vogelenzang, Holland or FRANZ ROOZEN LTD. c/o Mrs. Sue
Evans, 34 Friars Road, Braughing, Ware, Herts SG11 2NN

WALTER BLOM & SON LTD., Coombelands Nurseries, Leavesden,
Watford, Herts WD2 7BH

P. DE JAGER AND SONS LTD., The Nurseries, Marden,
Kent TN12 9BP

VAN TUBERGEN U.K. LTD., Bressingham, Diss,
Norfolk IP22 2AB

J. PARKER DUTCH BULBS CO., 452 Chester Road, Old Trafford,
Manchester M16 9HL

JACQUES AMAND LTD., The Nurseries, Clamp Hill, Stanmore,
Middlesex HA7 3JS

BROADLEIGH GARDENS, Barr House, Bishops Hull, Taunton,
Somerset TA4 1AE

JACQUES BAKKER HOLLAND, P.O Box 111, Spalding,
Lincolnshire PE12 6EL

RUPERT BOWLBY, Gatton, Reigate, Surrey RH2 0TA

BRIAN DUNCAN, 'Knowehead', 15 Ballynahatty Road, Omagh,
Co. Tyrone, N. Ireland BT78 1PN

AVON BULBS, Upper Westwood, Bradford-on-Avon,
Wiltshire BA15 2AT

POTTERTON & MARTIN, Cottage Nursery, Moortown Rd,
Nettleton, Caistor, Lincs. LN7 6HX

CAMBRIDGE BULBS, 40 Whittlesford Road, Newton,
Cambridge CB2 5PH

W.E. TH. INGWERSEN LTD., Birch Farm, Gravetye,
Nr. East Grinstead, West Sussex RH19 4LE

PARADISE CENTRE, Twinstead Road, Lamarsh, Bures,
Suffolk CO8 5EX.

THOMPSON & MORGAN, London Road, Ipswich,
Suffolk IP2 0BA.

SUPPLIERS IN NORTH AMERICA

W. ATLEE BURPEE AND CO., 300 Park Avenue,
Warminster PA 18991–0003

P. DE JAGER & SONS BULBS INC., 188 Asbury Street,
P.O Box 2010, Hamilton, Mass. 01982

DUTCH GARDENS, P.O. Box 200, Adelphia, NJ 07710

HERITAGE GARDENS, 1 Meadow Ridge Road, Shenandoah,
Iowa 51601–0700

JACKSON AND PERKINS, 1 Rose Lane, Medford, OR 97501–9811

JOHN SCHEEPERS, INC., RD 6, Philipsburg Road, Middletown,
NY 10940

MCCLURE AND ZIMMERMAN, 108 West Winnebago,
P.O. Box 368, Friesland, WI 539235

NETHERLAND BULB COMPANY INC., 2 Cypress Peak Lane,
Montvale, NJ 07645

SMITH AND HAWKEN, 25 Corte Madera, Mill Valley, CA 94941

THOMPSON & MORGAN, P.O. Box 1308, Jackson, NJ 08527

K. VAN BOURGONDIEN BROS., 245 Farmingdale Rd., Route 109,
P.O. Box A, Babylon, NY 11702

VAN ENGELEN INC., Stillbrook Farm 313 Maple Street,
Litchfield, CT 06759

WAYSIDE GARDENS, 1 Garden Lane, Hodges, SC 29695–0001

WHITE FLOWER FARM, Litchfield, CT 06759–0050

BIBLIOGRAPHY

ARDÈNE, LE PÈRE (1765)   Traité des Tulipes Chambeau, Avignon

BAKER, ARTHUR (1931)   Cult of the Tulip in Turkey, Journal RHS

BECKMANN, J (1846)   History of Inventions and Discoveries, London

BLUNT, WILFRED (1950)   Tulipomania, Penguin, London

BLUNT, WILFRED (1977)   Tulips and Tulipomania, Basilisk Press, London (a reprint of 1950 edition with new illustrations)

BOTSCHANTZEVA, Z.P. (1982)   Tulips, Trans. H.Q. Varekamp, Balkema, Rotterdam

BOWLES, E.A. (1946)   My Favourite Tulips, Daffodil & Tulip Yearbook, RHS

CALVERT, H.V. (1970)   Florists' Tulips & the Wakefield & North of England Tulip Society, Daffodil & Tulip Year Book, RHS

CLUSIUS, C (1951)   A Treatise on Tulips, New ed. W van Dijk, Haarlem

DARLINGTON, C.D. & WYLIE, A.P. (1955)   Chromosome Atlas of Flowering Plants, Allen & Unwin, London

DIX, J.F.Ch. (1946)   Modern Tulip Developments, Daffodil & Tulip Year Book RHS

DIX J.F.Ch. (1951)   Tulipa Fosteriana & its Hybrids, Daffodil & Tulip Year Book RHS

DIX J.F.Ch. (1974)   De Veredeling van Tulpen, K.A.V.B. Hillegom

DYKES, W.R. (1925)   Some Wild Species of Tulip, Journal RHS

DYKES, W.R. (1930)   Notes on Tulip Species, H. Jenkins, London

FRIJLINK, A. (1954)   The Tulip, I Its Early History, II The Development of the Modern Tulip, Garden Journal, N.Y. Botanical Garden

HAKLUYT, RICHARD (1589)   Principal Navigations (New Ed. 1904) Glasgow

HALL, A.D. (1929)   The Book of the Tulip, Hopkinson, London

HALL, A.D. (1935)   Species of Tulipa for the Garden, Journal RHS

HALL, A.D. (1940)   The Genus Tulipa, RHS, London

HANDBOOK ON BULBS (1959)   Brooklyn Botanic Garden

HOOG, M.H. (1974)   De Oorsprong van de Tulipa, K.A.V.B. Hillegom

HOOG, M.H. (1976)   De Wilde Tulpen van Europa, Bloembollen-cultuur 86/36

INGWERSEN, W. (1951)   Using Bulbs in the Rock Garden, Gardens & Gardening

JACOB, REV. J. (1912)   Tulips, Jack, London & Edinburgh

KADEN, V. (1982)   The Illustration of Plants and Gardens, V. and A. Museum, London

KRELAGE, E.H. (1942)   Bloemenspeculatie in Nederland, Amsterdam

KRELAGE, E.H. (1946)   Drie Eeuwen Bloembollenexport, The Hague

KRELAGE, E.H. (1951)   Historical Tulip in Literature, Daffodil Tulip Year Book RHS

LODEWIJK, T. (1978)   The Book of Tulips, Cassell, London

MALO, C. (c1830)   Histoire des Tulipes, Paris

MARAIS, W. (1980)   Notes on Tulipa, Kew Bulletin, London

MONSTEREUL, LA CHESNÉE (1654)   Le Floriste François, Caen

MURRAY, W.S. (1909)   Tulips and Tulipomania, Journal RHS

NEWTON, W.C.F. (1927)   Chromosome studies in Tulipa, J.Linn Soc. Bot.

PARKINSON, JOHN (1629)   Paradisi in Sole Paradisus Terrestris London

REPORT (1917)   of the Tulip Nomenclature Committee of the RHS

RICHERT, A. (1980)   Le Jardin de Tulipes, Neuilly-sur-Seine

SELDEN, M.M. (1942)   Ups and Downs of Tulip Bulbs, National Washington

SLOGTEREN, E. VAN (1947)   The Preparing of Tulips for Early Forcing, Daffodil & Tulip Year Book RHS

SLOGTEREN, D.H. VAN AND ASJES, C.J. (1970)   Virus Diseases in Tulips, Daffodil & Tulip Year Book RHS

SOLMS-LAUBACH, H. GRAF ZU (1899)   Weizen und Tulpe, Felix Leipzig

SOUTHERN, D.I. (1967)   Species Relationships in the Genus Tulipa Berlin

STAFLEU, F.A. (1963)   The Tulip and the Netherlands, Garden J. N.Y. Bot. Garden

STORK, A.L. (1979)   Tulipes Botaniques, Rev. Hort. Suisse

STORK, A.L. (1983)   Tulipes de Samarkand etc. Rev. Hort. Suisse

STORK, A.L. (1984)   Tulipes Sauvages et Cultvées, Geneva

STOUT, A.B. (1919)   Tulip Droppers, J. Int. Gard. Club, New York

SWEET, R. (1829–32)   The Florist's Guide, London

VVEDENSKII, A.I. (1949)   Key to the Tulips of the USSR, Daffodil & Tulip Year Book RHS

VVEDENSKII, A.I. (1968)   Tulipa L. in Flora of the USSR, Jerusalem

WENDELBO, P. (1977)   Tulips and Irises of Iran, Tehran

WRIGHT, M. (1957)   A Garden of Ten Million Bulbs, Gard. J. New York Bot. Garden

ZAITSEVA, E.N. (1958)   Tyul'pany (Tulips) Moscow

INDEX

ACKNOWLEDGEMENTS

Cathy Wilkinson Barash: pp121; 13; 16; 18; 20, 22bl; 22tr; 24; 25; 26tl; 26bl; 27cl; 27bl; 28; 30br; 30bl; 31; 32; 34; 35br; 35tr; 36; 37l; 37cr; 38; 39; 40; 41l; 44; 45; 46; 47; 48; 49; 50; 52; 53tr; 53br; 53bl; 56l; 58; 59; 60; 61; 62; 63; 64; 65r; 66; 68; 69; 70t; 71; 75br; 76b; 84b; 85; 86tl; 89bl; 89tr; 90t; 92; 93t; 94; 96; 97; 98l; 106; 107t; 113; 114; 115r; 116l; 119; 123. **John Killingback**: pp6; 56r; 72; 74; 75tr; 78;; 100; 101; 102; 103; 104tr; 116r; 117; 118; 122. **Stanley Killingback**: pp11; 14; 17; 19; 77; 80b; 84r; 98r 110; 115l. **Elvin McDonald**: pp12r; 22br; 33; 83b; 88r; 90b; 91; 99; 108; 112. **Courtesy, Netherlands Flowerbulb Information Centre**: pp26r; 27tl; 27r; 30tl; 35tl; 37tr; 37br; 41r; 42; 53tl; 65l; 67; 70b; 75tl; 76t; 79bl; 79tl; 80t; 81; 82r; 83t; 89tl; 93br; 93bl; 107b. **Ann Reilly/Photonats**: pp79r; 82l; 84t. **Harry Smith Horticultural Photographic Collection**: p54.

r=right, l=left, c=center, t=top, b=bottom